the

MR. X INTERVIEWS

Volume 2

WORLD VIEWS FROM A
FICTIONAL US SOVEREIGN CREDITOR

LUKE GROMEN

AVIVA
PUBLISHING
New York

The Mr. X Interviews, Volume 2: World Views from a Fictional
US Sovereign Creditor

Copyright © 2020 by Luke Gromen. All rights reserved.

Published by:
Aviva Publishing
Lake Placid, NY
(518) 523-1320
www.AvivaPubs.com

Address all inquiries to:
Luke Gromen
info@fftt-llc.com
440-732-0764
www.FFTT-LLC.com

ISBN: 978-1-890427-28-3

Library of Congress Control Number: 2018912681

Editor: Tyler Tichelaar/Superior Book Productions
Design & Layout: Birte Kahrs

Every attempt has been made to source all quotes properly.
First Edition

To my wife and my three sons,

my mom and dad,

Kathy McGinnis,

and to everyone I've met on this journey.

Thank you.

CONTENTS

ACKNOWLEDGMENTS

"Mr. X" is a composite of a number of historical figures and modern-day people. A heartfelt thank you to you all.

DISCLOSURES

FFTT, LLC ("FFTT", Forest for the Trees) is an independent research firm. FFTT's reports are based upon information gathered from various sources believed to be reliable but not guaranteed as to accuracy or completeness. The analysis or recommendations contained in the reports, if any, represent the true opinions of the author. The views expressed in the reports are not knowingly false and do not omit material facts that would make them misleading. No part of the author's compensation was, is, or will be, directly or indirectly, related to the specific recommendations or views about any and all of the subject securities or issuers. However, there are risks in investing. Any individual report is not all-inclusive and does not contain all of the information you may desire in making an investment decision. You must conduct and rely on your own evaluation of any potential investment and the terms of its offering, including the merits and risks involved in making a decision to invest.

The information in this report is not intended to be, and shall not constitute, an offer to sell or a solicitation of an offer to buy any security or investment product or service. The information in this report is subject to change without notice, and FFTT assumes no responsibility to update the information contained in this report. The author, company, and/or its individual officers, employees, or members of their families might, from time to time, have a position in the securities mentioned and may purchase or sell these securities in the future. The author, company, and/or its individual officers, employees, or members of their families might, from time to time, have financial interests with affiliates of companies whose securities have been discussed in this publication.

"It's important to understand many important stories are always hiding in the open."

— Seymour Hersh, Pulitzer Prize Winning Reporter

Chapter 1

CHINESE YUAN BEARS SEEM TO BE MISSING SOMETHING CRITICAL

OCTOBER 2017

My iPhone rang; I turned it over to see a familiar foreign country code. It was Mr. X.

"Hello, my friend!" I greeted him, excited to hear his voice.

"Luke, how are you?"

"I'm well, Mr. X. And you?"

"I'm excellent. Listen, I hate to be brief, but I am going to be in New York next week. I apologize for the short notice, but would you be able to join me for dinner next Thursday? There is much to discuss."

I quickly toggled over to my Outlook calendar and found it wide open. "I'm available. Thursday night, same place as usual? What time?" I asked.

"Seven o'clock?" Mr. X suggested.

"Perfect," I replied. "See you then."

When the day came, I touched down at LaGuardia in the morning, met a dear friend for lunch, and saw clients before heading downtown to the restaurant in Chelsea. Mr. X was waiting for me, and he rose to meet me when I walked in.

Luke: Thank you for inviting me to dinner. It's great to see you again.

Mr. X: You're welcome; thank you for joining me. I've been excited to catch up.

Luke: You usually have provocative observations about global markets you are willing to share—anything grabbing your attention these days?

Mr. X: Yes. A number of high-profile investors are negative on China and the Chinese yuan (CNY), based on analyzing China using traditional Emerging Market (EM) Balance of Payments (BoP) metrics. However, in one critical aspect, China is no longer an EM, yet these investors are analyzing China as if it still is; that may prove to be a grave error.

Luke: What do you mean? In what critical aspect is China no longer an EM?

Mr. X: Historically, under the petrodollar system, EMs had to run current account surpluses (earn USDs on net) in order to buy oil and other commodities and to service any USD-denominated debt. In instances where EMs began to run deficits, they had to sell FX reserves to support their currencies; when they ran out of FX reserves, they suffered a currency crisis where their currency fell sharply versus the US dollar (Russia 1998, SE Asia 1997, Argentina 2001, etc.)

If oil and commodities are only priced in USDs, the only way for the EMs to move from a current account deficit to a surplus once they run out of FX reserves to support their currency is by devaluing their currency. China/CNY bears are looking at China through this lens, but they are missing something very important in my view.

8

Luke: Which is what?

Mr. X: The bear case on CNY rests squarely on the assumption that China is subject to that same aforementioned EM calculus. China imports a lot of oil, and it will likely need to import even more in the coming years.

Furthermore, the IEA (International Energy Agency) recently increased global oil demand estimates [See chart below, source: IEA].

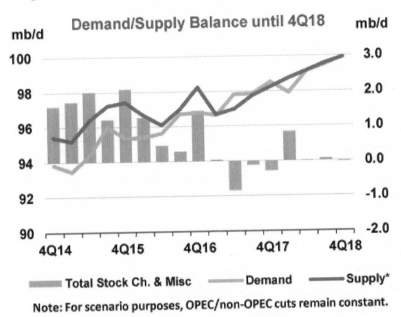

Note: For scenario purposes, OPEC/non-OPEC cuts remain constant.

Importantly, all of this will be happening in the context of global energy industry capital spending having been slashed by more than $1 trillion over the past 2-3 years during the oil downturn.

[Mr. X passed to me the following article:
Global oil industry capex cuts top $1T – 6/15/16

https://www.cnbc.com/2016/06/15/global-oil-industrys-retrenchment-tops-a-staggering-1-trillion.html]

Given the above factors, if we look at China through the traditional EM lens as CNY bears do, we see that as Chinese oil imports and the price of oil begin to rise, China will move toward running a current account deficit, in the presence of a highly-levered banking system, which will force China to bleed down FX reserves to below some critical level, at which point China will then have to significantly devalue the CNY. We have seen numerous EMs go through this exact situation during the last 30-40 years.

Luke: That seems to make sense to me…but I take it you disagree?

Mr. X: Oh, yes. In my opinion, this analysis ignores a critical development.

Luke: How?

Mr. X: It's only valid if oil is only priced in USDs. Then the CNY bears may very well be proven right—China could suffer the traditional EM currency crisis, necessitating the CNY devaluation the CNY bears are looking for.

However, if oil begins being priced in CNY, then the CNY bears will likely be waiting a long, long time for the big CNY devaluation they think is imminent….

Luke: Why?

Mr. X: Because the upcoming CNY oil contract in the presence of what is essentially a reopened "Bretton Woods gold window at a floating price through CNY" will give China a second lever to manage its current account with—a second lever that no other EM in history has ever had to manage its current account with. This is the critical aspect most CNY bears are missing that I mentioned earlier. They appear to be totally ignoring the implications of this reality.

Luke: I don't understand how pricing oil in CNY or a CNY oil contract changes anything.

Mr. X: Pricing oil in CNY in the presence of an open gold window through CNY changes everything! Once China has a CNY oil contract (if it has even a modest degree of success), then whenever rising Chinese oil imports or rising oil prices begin to push the Chinese current account toward a deficit position (historically catastrophic for an EM), China can simply act in markets to increase the gold/oil ratio (GOR) it and its oil suppliers transact oil at, which gives China complete control over its energy bill. It will be the first and only EM ever to have had such power. They talked about doing this two years ago:

[Mr. X passed to me the following article:

> **China likely to get nod for CNY gold fix soon, could compel foreign suppliers to pay "local CNY price" - 6/24/15**
>
> http://mobile.reuters.com/article/idUSKBN0P40D5201506 24?irpc=932]

Luke: I don't understand—what would be the benefit of China increasing the GOR with its oil suppliers?

Mr. X: It would give China full control over its oil import bill, which will allow it to lower its oil import bill and, therefore, increase its current account surplus, whenever it sees fit...and critically, China will be able to do this without having to devalue its currency, as the CNY bears are expecting.

Luke: How do you know that will happen?

Mr. X: Because I watched it happen in 2014-15!

Look at these charts. (Mr. X showed me the charts to the right and below.) Back in 2014, China's current account surplus was heading toward a deficit, and then it opened SGEI (Shanghai International Gold Exchange) in the third quarter of 2014 and the GOR blew out (through a collapse in oil prices), driving a sharp rebound in China's current account surplus as its oil import bill collapsed:

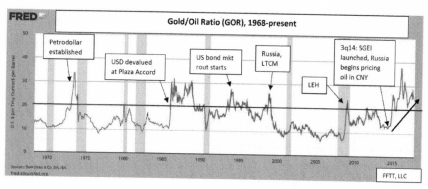

Luke: But didn't China still have to devalue the CNY in the third quarter of 2015? Why did they do that?

Mr. X: Yes, they did, modestly. I'm not exactly sure why, but it is important to note they did not have a CNY oil contract then. However, I'm hearing that they likely will soon…and I'm further hearing that the CNY will indeed be fully convertible under the oil contract, which will make it easier for China—or perhaps the PBOC (People's Bank of China)?—to adjust the GOR to manage China's current account without having to significantly devalue its currency any further.

Luke: Interesting. Is oil the only commodity China would be able to do this for?

Mr. X: Great question. [Mr. X passed me the chart below.] As best I can tell from the data from this MIT database, somewhere near 50 percent of China's $1.3T in annual imports are commodities, all of which could at some point be subject to the same dynamic I just described in regards to oil—if they are priced only in USD and they rise in price, and/or China buys more of them over time, it will push China toward a current account deficit and a classic EM currency crisis unless….

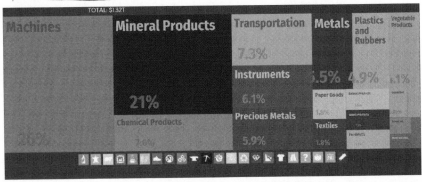

Source: http://atlas.media.mit.edu/en/profile/country/chn/

Luke: Unless China also begins to price those commodities in CNY as well.

Mr. X: Exactly. So, Luke, tell me: What do we think will happen over the next few years as say $650B of annual Chinese commodity purchases are increasingly done in CNY, some sizable portion of which will likely be recycled into physical gold markets of which total annual global mine production is approximately $120B (and only approximately $90B ex-China and ex-Russia, since those countries aren't selling their domestic mine production externally)?

Luke: It would seem a pretty epic mismatch is developing.

Mr. X: Indeed. What this implies is that post-CNY oil contract launch, China will not have to devalue CNY in order to increase its current account surplus. It will only need to increase the GOR with critical oil suppliers.

Furthermore, to the extent China's current account may move closer to deficit in coming months/quarters per the earlier chart from Brad Setser at the Council on Foreign Relations (CFR), China may be incentivized to increase the GOR sooner rather than later. At the very least, this will likely continue to keep USD oil prices from rising unless USD gold prices rise significantly first, and it may put renewed pressure on oil prices if gold doesn't rise. Lastly, as the world begins to realize what is happening here, it is likely going to want to start owning physical gold.

Luke: Do you think the world is beginning to realize "what is happening here," as you say?

Mr. X: A number of hints suggest that yes, a number of others in the world (besides you Luke!) are starting to realize what is happening. Here are some articles that reflect that. [Mr. X handed me the following list.]

China aims for dollar-free oil trade – 9/14/17

https://asia.nikkei.com/magazine/20170914/Business/China
-aims-for-dollar-free-oil-trade

**PBOC official says China is keen to promote the use of
CNY in commodity pricing – 9/19/17**

http://www.scmp.com/news/china/economy/article/211189
2/central-bank-official-says-china-keen-promote-use-yuan-
commodity

**China will compel Saudi to trade oil in CNY, that will
affect USD – 10/11/17**

https://www.cnbc.com/2017/10/11/china-will-compel-
saudi-arabia-to-trade-oil-in-yuan--and-thats-going-to-
affect-the-us-dollar.html

**Saxo Bank: USD reserve status is at risk as China de-
dollarizes – 10/11/17**

https://www.cnbc.com/2017/10/11/the-us-dollar-may-be-at-
risk-as-the-global-reserve-currency.html

> China is eyeing the benefits of having its own
> currency play a larger role & to supplant the USD's
> role in global trade…the initial focus is on the
> global oil trade, where it has announced the
> intention of buying oil in CNY & allowing trade
> partners to settle that CNY in gold.

**Oil for gold—the real story: Alasdair Macleod –
10/12/17**

https://www.goldmoney.com/research/goldmoney-
insights/oil-for-gold-the-real-story

**Curran—The petrodollar system is being undermined:
Barron's – 10/14/17**

http://www.barrons.com/articles/the-coming-renaissance-of-macro-investing-1507957012?mg=prod/accounts-barrons

Another major secular change that is under way in the oil market comes from the geopolitical arena. China, now the world's largest importer of oil, is no longer comfortable purchasing oil in a currency over which it has no control, and has taken the following steps that allow it to circumvent the use of the U.S. dollar:

1. China has agreed with Russia to purchase Russian oil and natural gas in CNY.

2. As an example of China's newfound power to influence oil exporters, China has persuaded Angola (the world's second-largest oil exporter to China) to accept the CNY as legal tender, evidence of efforts made by Beijing to speed up internationalization of the CNY. The incredible growth rates of the Chinese economy and its thirst for oil have endowed it with tremendous negotiating strength that has led, and will lead, other countries to cater to China's needs at the expense of their historical client, the U.S.

3. China is set to launch an oil exchange by the end of the year that is to be settled in CNY. Note that in conjunction with the existing Shanghai Gold Exchange, also denominated in CNY, any country will now be able to trade and hedge oil, circumventing USD transactions, with the flexibility to take payment in CNY or gold, or exchange gold into any global currency.

China's CNY oil contract plans will be a 'wakeup call' to investors who haven't paid attention: Levinson – 10/24/17

https://www.bloomberg.com/news/articles/2017-10-24/graticule-s-levinson-sees-wake-up-call-from-china-s-oil-plans

Mr. X: Some big and very non-tin-foil-hat wearing investors and banks are seeing that China is working to gain the ability to price commodities in their own currency. In my experience, that is often a clue that the herd is coming. Other clues suggest the US government has noticed that China is working to price commodities in its own currency (and as a result, working to undermine the petrodollar system) as well.

Luke: Such as?

Mr. X: Well, we can infer that the US government had to have been aware of this situation as far back as 2014 based on these comments from "people who would know." [Mr. X pulled out another sheet of paper and read the following to me.]

> American media seems to be focused on domestic affairs while astonishing things are going on beyond the borders— and we seem to stand by watching helplessly. The United States' position of prominence is eroding.

> Yesterday, at a summit in Shanghai between China's President Xi Jinping and Russian President Vladimir Putin a massive 30-year natural gas deal was signed to provide Russian gas to China. The agreement has been under negotiation for years and its fruition is a big deal for energy markets and international politics.

> Less noticed, but possibly even more interesting, was an agreement between Russia and China aimed at undermining the role of the US dollar as the base currency.

The Russian bank VTB and the Bank of China signed an agreement in the presence of Xi and Putin to avoid using the dollar and conduct exchanges in domestic currencies. This is a really big signal. The all mighty dollar may not always be all mighty.

[As he read, Mr. X's tone emphasized certain points to make sure I didn't miss them.]

Look at the world (or even just the United States) from the position of China. What makes America a super power? Is it the military? Partly. Is it nuclear weapons? Not so much. What really gives us leverage is the position of the dollar as the base currency. In the last financial crisis, we escaped largely by printing money. Other countries can't get away with that without causing massive inflation.

Sitting in Beijing, it could be seen as a financial attack— US Treasury printing tons of dollars that has the effect of exporting inflation to other countries. We borrow money (by selling treasuries to finance our wars, debt, TARP, etc.) and then pay them off by, in essence, printing dollars.

The role of the dollar as base currency is a uniquely powerful lever. It is one that is rarely thought of in terms of national security, but nothing is more important. If we lose it, we will have lost our position as the last super power. Period.

Beijing, Moscow, and others are well aware of this. The role of the dollar also gives us the currently valuable tool of sanctions. If Washington decides to limit banking use of dollars for transactions with certain entities, e.g. in Russia or Iran, then we can impose our will on the international financial system. You can bet there is no higher strategic priority than to undermine that position.

We are blindly squandering this leverage from inattention and by our inability to control our appetite for printed dollars. This is a national security issue, not just a budget issue.

American Vulnerability—The Dollar: Charles Duelfer - May 22, 2014

http://www.charlesduelfer.com/blog/?p=239

> [Charles Duelfer spent over 25 years in the national security agencies of the US government. He was involved in policy development, operations, & intelligence in the Middle East, Africa, Central America, & Asia.]

...gold is being moved in sort of unique ways, concentrated and secret and unique ways, and capitals are slowly but surely and methodically divesting themselves of US Treasuries. That Beijing and Moscow are both complicit in this, and what they're trying to do is weaken the dollar.

What they want to do is use Putin and others' oil power, petrodollars if you will, and I say that petro-yuan, petro-renminbi, petro-euro, whatever, to force the United States to lose its incredibly powerful role of owning the world's transactional reserve currency.

Lawrence Wilkerson, former Chief of Staff to Sec. State Colin Powell, 10/8/14

https://www.youtube.com/watch?v=YM_MH_Bfq5c

Mr. X: More recently, Secretary of State Rex Tillerson gave what was, in my mind, a clear hint that the US government is both well-aware of what is happening, and that they are none-too-happy about it. [Mr. X passed me the following article.]

> **Tillerson accuses China of undermining the "international, rules-based order" over North Korea – 10/19/17**
>
> https://www.bloomberg.com/amp/news/articles/2017-10-19/tillerson-signals-impatience-with-china-on-north-korea-trade

Luke: But wasn't Tillerson talking about Chinese moves regarding North Korea, not about Chinese moves to circumvent the petrodollar?

Mr. X: Yes, but in my view, those comments were akin to Secretary of State Colin Powell talking about Iraq regarding Iraqi WMDs, not about Iraq's move to circumvent the petrodollar by pricing oil in EURs instead of USDs.

Luke: Touché. Okay, so I get all of that, but here's what I don't get: If China reopens a gold window through CNY at a floating price in an attempt to print CNY first for oil and eventually for up to $650B in annual Chinese commodity imports v. just $120B in gold globally mined annually, won't this just either:

1. **Create a run on Chinese gold, emptying out their vaults, or**
2. **Bid up CNY gold, devaluing CNY v. the USD through the gold link?**

Mr. X: No.

Luke: Why not?

Mr. X: Because China learned from the US' mistakes under Bretton Woods how *not* to operate an open gold window.

Luke: What do you mean?

Mr. X: China is *not* fixing the price of gold like the US did (US mistake #1), and China has made it so that mainland China gold *cannot* leave China—this means that when Russia, Iran, Saudi, or others eventually show up in Shanghai, Hong Kong, or perhaps even London, with offshore CNY, demanding physical gold settlement for some portion of their offshore CNY, that gold will have to come from somewhere other than China, unlike what the US did (shipping US gold to satisfy USD obligations was US mistake #2 under Bretton Woods).

Luke: Okay, so run me through how this would actually work to make sure I understand—let's say I am Russia, and I have CNY from selling oil to China. I show up in Shanghai at the Shanghai Gold Exchange International Board (SGEI), or in Hong Kong, or even London, and ask for gold?

Mr. X: Yes.

Luke: Then what?

Mr. X: Then gold must be sourced...but it *cannot* by law come from mainland China. It must come from somewhere else. As a practical matter, that means either the UK, the US, or India...but the Indians aren't selling much gold at these prices, are they? (Smiling.)

Luke: No, the Indians are not. Okay, so then the physical gold to deliver to a holder of offshore CNY must come from the UK or the US. Then what?

Mr. X: Then the UK and/or US gold markets answer China's request for gold one of three ways:

1. *"Yes, we will deliver you gold, but we will not let the price of gold rise by allowing paper gold market leverage to rise in London and NYC.* (i.e., we deliver you gold but sell more paper gold obligations to keep gold's price from rising and,

21

thereby, prevent your gold purchases from devaluing the USD via a rising gold price.)"

2. *"Yes, we will deliver you gold, and we will let gold's price rise as a result of your purchases.* (i.e., we will allow foreign purchases of CNY gold in Asia to devalue the USD via a rising gold price.)"

3. *"No, you cannot have gold. We either refuse to deliver it or we are out of gold."* If this happens, force majeure will be declared and China/Russia will reset the gold price to whatever level they see fit...which will likely significantly devalue the USD via a rising gold price.

Luke: Oh, my God...I get it. China and Russia have the USD in checkmate, just as Wilkerson and Duelfer publicly feared over three years ago, but most Western investors do not realize it because they pay no attention to physical gold.

Mr. X: Exactly...and also because Western investors generally ignore history books. What I'm describing to you is simply a version of the London Gold Pool breakdown in the late 1960s and subsequent US closing of the gold window in 1971 under President Nixon.

Back then, it was a run on US gold by the US' EU creditors, who decided they no longer wanted to fund the Vietnam War and LBJ's Great Society deficits. They demanded their gold back at $42, and despite all that demand, gold prices never budged...until the window was closed. Then gold rose twenty times in the next eight years.

Essentially, China is doing the same thing this time, which makes sense since China has been the biggest marginal foreign financier of US deficits for the past fifteen years since its UST (US

Treasury) holdings have gone from $60B in 2001 to $1.3T by 2011.

Apparently not that many investors in the US have read the history of what happened in the 1960s that led to the 1970s inflation and USD weakness...which is too bad because they may be caught by surprise if, or more likely when, something directionally similar happens again.

Luke: Yes, they will...and it seems to me that when it happens, it may happen rather quickly.

Mr. X: These sorts of things have a way of doing that. You know, like Hemingway wrote, "First I went broke slowly, and then all at once."

Luke: Why don't we stop there for today then. Thank you again for your time and your thoughts, Mr. X. It is always great catching up with you.

Mr. X: It's been my pleasure.

Chapter 2

CHINA THREATENS TO CEASE BUYING USTS IN RESPONSE TO TRADE TENSIONS—MR. X'S THOUGHTS

JANUARY 2018

Three months after our meeting in New York, Mr. X and I caught up again, this time for dinner in Chicago, where Mr. X had flown to meet with some of his business partners. The flight for me from Cleveland to Chicago was an easy one, and I looked forward to discussing newly-developing events with him.

Luke: Mr. X, it is great to see you again. First, let me ask you what I'm sure everyone wants to ask you: What's your take on China's announced and subsequently denied statement about slowing or halting UST purchases?

[I handed Mr. X two articles to clarify what I was referring to.]

> **China weighs slowing or halting UST purchases – 1/10/18**
>
> https://www.bloomberg.com/news/articles/2018-01-10/china-officials-are-said-to-view-treasuries-as-less-attractive

China denies it intends to reduce UST purchases – 1/11/18

https://www.ft.com/content/924e4c88-f692-11e7-88f7-5465a6ce1a00

Mr. X: (Smiling) What was it that Otto von Bismarck said, "Never believe anything in politics until it has been officially denied"? Perhaps that's apropos in this case. Regardless, I have had a number of thoughts on it.

My first thought was that the initial headline seemed redundant because the reality is that China has not bought a single UST on a net basis since late 2013 when the PBOC announced it was no longer in China's interest to stockpile FX reserves.

[He handed me the following article.]

PBOC says no longer in China's interest to boost FX reserves 11/20/13

https://www.bloomberg.com/news/articles/2013-11-20/pboc-says-no-longer-in-china-s-favor-to-boost-record-reserves

My next thought was that it would seem China is finally responding to US threats in a predictable manner.

Luke: What US threats? And what do you mean when you say "China is responding in a predictable manner"?

Mr. X: Well, we have seen a number of senior US officials threaten China in recent months.

[He handed me the following list of articles to prove his point.]

Mnuchin threatens banning China from "dollar system" (SWIFT) – 9/12/17

https://www.bloomberg.com/news/articles/2017-09-12/mnuchin-threatens-financial-sanctions-on-china-over-north-korea

Tillerson accuses China of undermining the "international, rules-based order" over North Korea – 10/19/17

https://www.bloomberg.com/amp/news/articles/2017-10-19/tillerson-signals-impatience-with-china-on-north-korea-trade

Trump to accuse China of 'economic aggression': FT – 12/17/17

https://www.ft.com/content/1801d4f4-e201-11e7-8f9f-de1c2175f5ce

> HR McMaster, US national security adviser who oversaw the strategy, this week said China—along with Russia—was a "revisionist power" that was "undermining the international order."

US to decide on trade sanctions against China this month – 1/10/18

https://asia.nikkei.com/Politics-Economy/International-Relations/US-to-decide-on-trade-sanctions-against-China-this-month

Mr. X: Furthermore, I say that China is responding in a predictable manner because both former US Secretary of State Kerry and former US President Obama warned us in a ten-day time span in August 2015 how China might respond to any such threats. Here is what President Obama said on August 5, 2015. [Again, Mr. X emphasized what he thought were the key points]:

We cannot dictate the foreign, economic and energy policies of every major power in the world. In order to even try to do that, *we would have to sanction, for example, some of the world's largest banks. We'd have to cut off countries like China from the American financial system.*

And since they happen to be major purchasers of our debt, *such actions could* trigger severe disruptions in our own economy, and, by the way, *raise questions internationally about the dollar's role as the world's reserve currency.* That's part of the reason why many of the previous unilateral sanctions were waived.

As an aside, it would appear to my eyes that perhaps it did not take long for Washington to get China's message.

Luke: Why do you say that?

Mr. X: Because this story hit Reuters news wires mere hours after China's surprising UST announcement:

> BREAKING: Trump's top advisers to recommend he extend Iran relief from sanctions by Friday deadline, though he is reluctant. — Senior official

Luke: How about that for quick response…interesting. So, to get back to your original point, if China hasn't bought any USTs on a net basis since 2013, when it announced (for the first time apparently) that it would no longer add to FX reserves (essentially code for "USTs"), why do you think this announcement was leaked yesterday? [I passed him the following chart.]

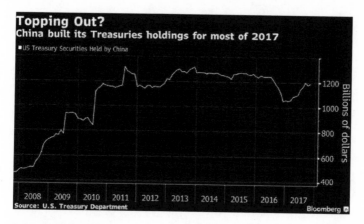

Topping Out?
China built its Treasuries holdings for most of 2017

Mr. X: I think it's a big signpost of where China thinks it is in the process of de-dollarizing the global commodity markets. To me, this was a subtle warning from China.

Luke: I'm no expert in Chinese culture, but in my limited readings, that's the sense I've gotten as well. That begs the question: Why did they resend this message now, and in the manner it was conveyed?

Mr. X: I think China feels it's being pushed too far or too aggressively, and perhaps more importantly, the letter suggests China feels it is ready to do something about it. Do you know what "Chekhov's gun" is?

Luke: No, what is that?

Mr. X: It refers to the Russian nineteenth-century playwright Anton Chekhov who set clear rules about storytelling. According to Wikipedia:

> "Chekhov's gun is a dramatic principle that states that every element in a story must be necessary, and irrelevant elements should be removed; elements should not appear to make "false promises" by never coming into play. The statement is recorded in letters by Anton Chekhov several times, with some variation:

"Remove everything that has no relevance to the story. If you say in the first chapter that there is a rifle hanging on the wall, in the second or third chapter it absolutely must go off. If it's not going to be fired, it shouldn't be hanging there."

Luke: That sounds like Hank Paulson's "bazooka" from summer 2008! So, what's your point?

Mr. X: (Laughing) Yes, I guess it does, although I think Paulson was hoping *not* to have to fire it. My point is this: China will reportedly launch its CNY oil contract as early as next week, and once it is launched, China will begin to cease being an EM for all intents and purposes. [Mr. X handed me the following article.]

> **How China will shake up the oil futures market with launch of CNY oil futures – 1/1/18**
>
> https://www.bloomberg.com/news/articles/2018-01-01/how-china-will-shake-up-the-oil-futures-market-quicktake-q-a

Luke: What do you mean "China will cease being an EM for all intents and purposes"?

Mr. X: As we discussed in October when we last talked, if China can price critical commodities in its own currency that it can print, then it is no longer at serious risk of an EM currency crisis driven by a commodity import-driven balance-of-payments problem because having a CNY oil contract with CNY gold settlement will give China a second "lever" to manage its current account with. Instead of just bleeding down FX reserves as oil prices rise until China has an EM balance-of-payments crisis for lack of USDs available to buy oil, China will now be able to simply change the GOR in CNY terms.

Luke: I don't understand how pricing oil in CNY or the CNY oil contract does that or changes anything.

Mr. X: Pricing oil in CNY in the presence of an open gold window through CNY changes everything! Once China has a CNY oil contract (if it has even a modest degree of success), then whenever rising Chinese oil imports or rising oil prices begin to push the Chinese current account toward a deficit position (historically catastrophic for an EM), China can simply act in markets to increase the GOR it and its oil suppliers transact oil at, which gives China complete control over its energy bill...the first and only such EM ever to have such a power. It talked about doing this two years ago. [Mr. X handed me the following article.]

China likely to get nod for CNY gold fix soon, could compel foreign suppliers to pay "local CNY price" - 6/24/15

http://mobile.reuters.com/article/idUSKBN0P40D5201506 24?irpc=932

Luke: I don't understand—what would China increasing the GOR with its oil suppliers do?

Mr. X: It gives China full control over its oil import bill, which will allow it to lower its oil import bill and, therefore, increase its current account surplus, whenever it sees fit...and critically, China will be able to do this without having to devalue its currency as the CNY bears are expecting. We've seen this in markets over the past three years:

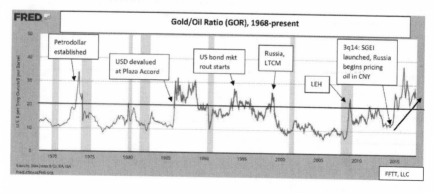

Luke: Knowing this then, is it looking like the CNY oil contract will be successful?

Mr. X: Early signs would seem to be encouraging. [He passed me the following list of articles supporting this point.]

Russia increases grip on Chinese oil market by opening 2nd ESPO pipeline doubling capacity to 600k bpd – 1/1/18

https://www.bloomberg.com/news/articles/2018-01-01/second-chinese-crude-oil-pipeline-linked-to-russia-s-espo-opens

Iran exports 784k bpd of oil to China in September, up 59% y/y – 10/25/17 [Note that it was all in CNY]

http://www.presstv.com/Detail/2017/10/25/539830/Irans-oil-exports-to-China-up-59

Saudis may seek funding in CNY – 8/24/17

https://www.reuters.com/article/us-saudi-china/saudis-may-seek-funding-in-chinese-yuan-idUSKCN1B413R

US lawmakers reach deal on new sanctions bill on Russia, Iran, North Korea – 7/22/17

https://www.reuters.com/article/us-usa-russia-sanctions/u-s-lawmakers-reach-deal-on-russia-sanctions-bill-creating-limits-for-trump-idUSKBN1A70L0

Mr. X: Additionally, I continue to hear that the profits from trading oil in CNY will be convertible into other currencies. And perhaps the most important signal was the one China sent yesterday. [He passed me another article.]

China weighs slowing or halting UST purchases – 1/10/18

https://www.bloomberg.com/news/articles/2018-01-10/china-officials-are-said-to-view-treasuries-as-less-attractive

Luke: Why do you think that's the most important signal?

Mr. X: Because in my opinion, "We don't need USTs anymore" equals "We are no longer at risk of a balance-of payments crisis anymore." Given the realities of China's trade balances, an EM-like balance-of-payments crisis would really be driven by Chinese commodity imports, so my read on this is that China's statement "We don't need USTs anymore" translates at its core to "We will soon be able to price oil and other commodities in our own currency to our satisfaction, control our own commodity import bill and, therefore, our own current account to our satisfaction."

Remember, as we discussed in October, as best as I can tell, somewhere near 50 percent of China's $1.3T in imports annually are commodities, all of which would be subject to the same dynamic we just described in regards to oil—if they are priced only in USD, and they rise in price and/or China buys more of them over time, it will push China toward a current account deficit and a classic EM currency crisis unless China can print CNY for them, and to my eyes, China seems to be making continued slow but steady progress on this front. [To back up this point, Mr. X gave me the following article.]

Pakistan official adopts CNY as trade currency after Trump tweet – 1/3/18

http://money.cnn.com/2018/01/03/news/economy/pakistan-china-trump-trade-yuan-dollar/index.html

Mr. X: I do find it humorous that the US media tries to spin this to claim Pakistan made such a significant change to trade policy in a tiny span of time in response to a Trump tweet. Doesn't it make more sense that Trump tweeted about it because it was already a done deal?

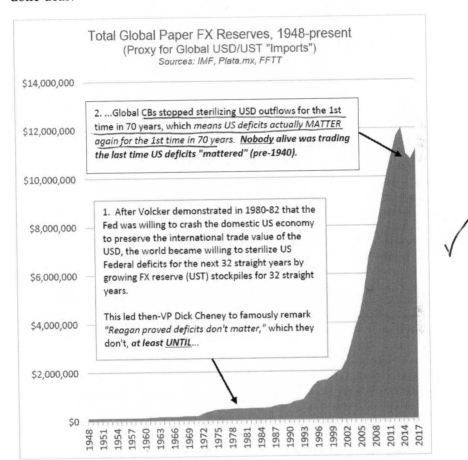

Total Global Paper FX Reserves, 1948-present
(Proxy for Global USD/UST "Imports")
Sources: IMF, Plata.mx, FFTT

2. ...Global CBs stopped sterilizing USD outflows for the 1st time in 70 years, which *means US deficits actually MATTER again for the 1st time in 70 years*. **Nobody** *alive was trading the last time US deficits "mattered" (pre-1940).*

1. After Volcker demonstrated in 1980-82 that the Fed was willing to crash the domestic US economy to preserve the international trade value of the USD, the world became willing to sterilize US Federal deficits for the next 32 straight years by growing FX reserve (UST) stockpiles for 32 straight years.

This led then-VP Dick Cheney to famously remark *"Reagan proved deficits don't matter,"* which they don't, *at least UNDER...*

Luke: So, what are the implications from here?

Mr. X: They are very straightforward, but most US investors I've talked to tend to see what appears to be happening as the "end of the world," but I think their perspective is skewed by their own experience of the past forty-five years.

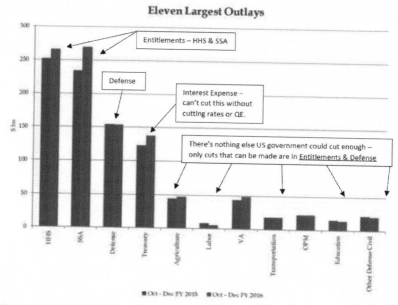

Eleven Largest Outlays

Source: United States Department of the Treasury

Luke: What do you mean?

Mr. X: This chart [He handed me the chart above] shows that when China stopped sterilizing USD outflows in 2014 (stockpiling FX reserves), something happened that had not happened in at least seventy years: Global FX reserve balances started falling.

Luke: What does that mean?

Mr. X: It means that for the first time in at least seventy years, US Federal deficits began to "matter again," to paraphrase something your former Vice President Dick Cheney reportedly said back in 2004 or 2005.

Luke: Which means…?

Mr. X: (Smiling) It means, in a way, "For the first time in at least seventy years, you Americans gotta start paying for your own stuff again."

Luke: What "stuff" do we have to pay for again?

Mr. X: Well, your Federal government's deficit is well over 100 percent of your nation's current account deficit, and your government spends the vast majority of its budget on just three line-items: entitlements, defense, and interest expense.

Luke: I don't get it.

Mr. X: What the PBOC told the world in 2013 and what I think China was gently reminding the world of yesterday was that it's not going to pay for US entitlements or defense spending anymore.

Luke: Okay, fine. We'll find someone else to pay for it. So what?

Mr. X: Luke, "someone else" *has* been paying for it since China and global central banks stopped doing so in the third quarter of 2014. Since global central banks stopped buying USTs then, the global private sector has been force-fed USTs like "financial *foie gras*"!

Luke: How do you know that?

Mr. X: Because that's what LIBOR (London Interbank Offered Rate) has been telling us since the third quarter of 2014. Remember in the fall of 2016 when Wall Street told us LIBOR would stop rising at around 90 basis points once Money Market Fund (MMF) Reforms went live in October of that year? Yeah, well, LIBOR just cut above 1.70 percent like a hot knife through butter and shows no signs of slowing down. [He passed me the following chart to illustrate his point.]

Luke: What is this telling us?

Mr. X: That your Federal government's deficits began crowding out the global private sector in the USD markets beginning in the third quarter of 2014 because "paying for your own stuff for the first time in at least seventy years" is really expensive. (smiling)

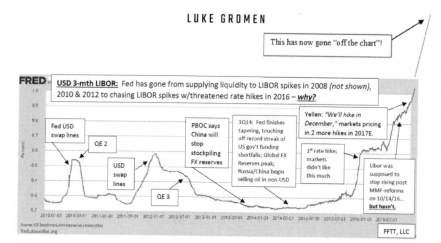

However, due to the USD's position as reigning global reserve currency, a significant negative for the US government and the USD actually drove the USD and LIBOR significantly *higher* as the US government effectively "scrambled to borrow from every source."

And by the way, I use those specific words, "scrambled to borrow from every source" *very* intently.

Luke: Why?

Mr. X: Because what began happening to the US in the third quarter of 2014 has happened before. It's just been a very long time, so most investors don't recognize it as it's been happening.

Luke: What do you mean "what began happening to the US in the third quarter of 2014 has happened before. It's just been a very long time"?

Mr. X: Reading about what happened to the biggest debtor in the world in the midst of the last global sovereign debt bubble is highly instructive; as you have frequently said, Luke, "History books are arguably the most undervalued assets on Wall Street." Let me share a quote from Liaquat Ahamed from page 125 of his book *Lords of Finance*. It refers to Rudolph Van Havenstein, who was president of Germany's Reichsbank in the early 1920s:

Von Havenstein faced a real dilemma. *Were he to refuse to print the money necessary to finance the deficit, he risked causing a sharp rise in interest rates as the government scrambled to borrow from every source.* The mass unemployment that would ensue, he believed, would bring on a domestic economic and political crisis, which in Germany's current fragile state might precipitate a real political convulsion. As the prominent Hamburg banker Max Warburg, a member of the Reichsbank's board of directors, put it, the dilemma was 'whether one wished to stop the inflation and trigger the revolution,' or continue to print money. Loyal servant of the state that he was, Von Havenstein had no wish to destroy the last vestiges of the old order.

Luke: Whoa, whoa, whoa! You're comparing the US' current situation to that of Germany in the immediate aftermath of World War I?

Mr. X: Directionally, yes. There are some important differences, but this part of the quote was quite apropos in my opinion: "Were he to refuse to print the money necessary to finance the deficit, he risked causing a sharp rise in interest rates as the government scrambled to borrow from every source." The Fed is going to be forced to do the same, much sooner than most investors think.

Luke: Why?

Mr. X: Germany lost a war. So has the US—the Global War on Terror hasn't gone so well.

Germany had a significant percentage of its manufacturing capacity seized by the Allies after the war, while the US has willingly offshored a significant percentage of its manufacturing capacity in response to "free trade deals" over the last twenty-five years.

That loss of German manufacturing capacity made it mathematically impossible for Germany to pay what were impossibly-large (as a percentage of German GDP), inflation-adjusting war reparations to the Allies in anything resembling real terms. Today, the offshoring of US manufacturing appears to have made it mathematically impossible for the US to pay impossibly-large (as a percentage of US GDP), inflation-adjusting entitlement obligations to its own people in anything resembling real terms.

The political situation in Germany post-World War I was, of course, far worse, but do tell me, Luke, is the domestic political situation in the US getting better or worse? More or less divided? (Smiling.)

Luke: You make some valid points, I guess. But how has the US "scrambled to borrow from every source," driving LIBOR higher?

Mr. X: You just have to know where to look and how to interpret headlines such as these, showing the US borrowing large amounts of money from US banks, from US MMFs (money market mutual funds), and from US citizens themselves. [He handed me the two articles below and the chart to the right.]

US regulators adopt tighter rules for banks' cash needs - 9/3/14

http://www.reuters.com/article/2014/09/03/financial-regulations-liquidity-idUSL1N0R414120140903?feedType=RSS&feedName=governmentFilingsNews

> The liquidity rules, which were first proposed in October 2013, will force banks to hold enough liquid assets such as cash, treasury bonds and other securities to fund themselves over a 30-day period during a crisis.

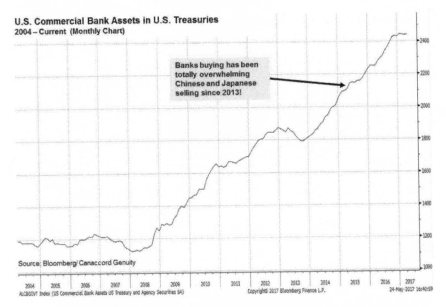

U.S. Commercial Bank Assets in U.S. Treasuries
2004 – Current (Monthly Chart)

Banks buying has been totally overwhelming Chinese and Japanese selling since 2013!

Source: Bloomberg/Canaccord Genuity

Money Market Fund changes driving borrowing costs sharply higher for cities, counties and companies – 8/8/16

http://www.wsj.com/articles/new-rules-and-fresh-headaches-for-short-term-borrowers-1470695795

Mr. X: The US also "scrambled to borrow" from its own citizens, as noted by the *Wall Street Journal* in a surprisingly-honest article published around the time your "Affordable Care Act" began to ramp up healthcare premiums for many Americans. [He read from the following article.]

More cost of healthcare shifts to consumers, helping Federal deficit – 12/3/14

http://www.wsj.com/articles/more-cost-of-health-care-shifts-to-consumers-1417640559

> While surveys show steeper out-of-pocket costs lead some people to defer even routine medical care, economists say the trend brings an important

upside: It is helping fuel a period of historically low growth in health-care spending, which eases the federal deficit.

"There has been a steady increase in deductibles and the main effect is to reduce use," said Drew Altman, president of the nonprofit Kaiser Family Foundation. "The gradual shift to consumers having more skin in the game is encouraged as part of national policy, and it's having an impact."

Luke: So you're saying....

Mr. X: I'm saying that if you look at the evidence the way it should be looked at, in my view, global Central Banks led by China began "choking out" US Federal government spending in the third quarter of 2014, and for the past three years, the US government has been "scrambling to borrow from every source," driving LIBOR much higher (and ironically taking the USD higher with it.)

Luke: But "choking out the US government's spending" is an act of financial war! Why doesn't the US respond?

Mr. X: (Laughing) What are they going to do—bomb Apple's factories in China? Hit Chinese targets with smart cruise missiles that use Chinese-sourced rare earth elements? Good luck with that.

Furthermore, to be clear, there are Chinese authorities who saw the US' implementation of Quantitative Easing (QE) in 2008 (instead of implementing the same draconian International Money Fund (IMF) Reforms imposed on every other nation that had suffered a similar crisis) as an act of financial war that started things.

Luke: Okay, fine, whatever. At the end of the day, we'll just keep both financing our deficits in the private sector *and* implementing policies that squeeze both LIBOR and the USD higher like we have done since 2014. Eventually, the strong

USD will break China just like it's broken every other EM in the past forty years.

Mr. X: Yes, you will, and you have. But that plan hit a snag in the third quarter of 2016.

Luke: What do you mean?

Mr. X: At some point on the path of "forcing the global private sector to finance US deficits driving higher rates and a stronger USD," the rising USD and rising interest rates triggered by US deficits crowding out the global private sector will begin to hurt the highly-financialized US economy. Once that happens, US tax receipts will begin falling as the US heads toward recession, and US deficits will begin rising as a percentage of GDP, which will then force the global private sector to finance even bigger US deficits, which will drive US tax receipts down even more and push the US economy down even closer to recession…wash, rinse, repeat. Critically, the point I just described was reached in the third quarter of 2016. [He passed me the following two charts.]

41

Luke: Wait, what?

Mr. X: In the third quarter of 2016, the US' "scrambling to borrow from every source" that had driven a higher USD and higher US rates since the third quarter of 2014 drove the US deficit to begin rising as a percentage of GDP for the first time since 2009:

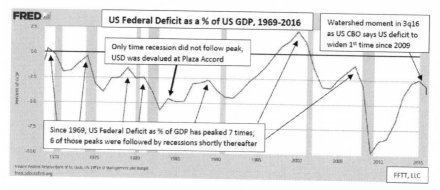

Luke: So, what you're saying is China led global central banks to begin "choking out" US Federal government spending in the third quarter of 2014 when it stopped increasing FX Reserve (UST) stockpiles, and the US "scrambled to borrow from every source" for two years, driving LIBOR (and the USD) sharply higher, and then in the third quarter of 2016, the first year-over-year drop in US tax receipts represented the US economy basically "tapping out"?

Mr. X: Yes, effectively. Beginning in the third quarter of 2016, the vortex shown in the diagram below began accelerating meaningfully:

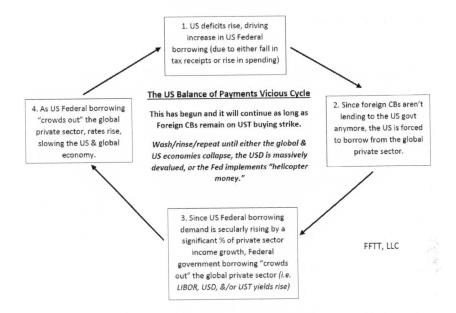

The US Balance of Payments Vicious Cycle

1. US deficits rise, driving increase in US Federal borrowing (due to either fall in tax receipts or rise in spending)

2. Since foreign CBs aren't lending to the US govt anymore, the US is forced to borrow from the global private sector.

3. Since US Federal borrowing demand is secularly rising by a significant % of private sector income growth, Federal government borrowing "crowds out" the global private sector (i.e. LIBOR, USD, &/or UST yields rise)

4. As US Federal borrowing "crowds out" the global private sector, rates rise, slowing the US & global economy.

This has begun and it will continue as long as Foreign CBs remain on UST buying strike.

Wash/rinse/repeat until either the global & US economies collapse, the USD is massively devalued, or the Fed implements "helicopter money."

FFTT, LLC

Luke: Oh my God...if this is true, what happens next?

Mr. X: With what happened in the third quarter of 2016 (deficit rising as a percentage of GDP), which sent the vortex above spinning faster, the US now has only four choices:

1. Go to war to force China and Russia to stop "choking out" US government spending.

2. Drastically cut US government spending on two of its three biggest expenditures: entitlements and defense (i.e., default on internal US obligations).

3. Drastically cut US government spending on the other biggest expenditure: interest expense (i.e., cut rates or default on external US obligations.)

4. Have the Fed "helicopter money" or use QE for the difference, or have the US Treasury significantly devalue the USD.

Luke: Which do you think is most likely?

Mr. X: Well, the only senior-level global central bank official who warned of the 2008 crisis ahead of time warned in the fourth quarter of 2016 that Option #4 (USD devaluation) would likely be the one chosen. [Mr. X quoted from the following article that he passed to me].

"We have run out of room on monetary policy" – William White, October 2016

http://www.lbma.org.uk/assets/events/Conference%202016/Speeches/Keynote%20Speech%20-%20White.pdf

> I am going to tell a less pleasant story...That is that we get an assumed slowdown or a global recession [Luke: This is the 2016 drop in US tax receipts.] Well, in that case...Efforts would be made to ensure that, somehow, you were forced to buy government bonds or maintain liquidity ratios [Luke: This is what the US has done to US banks, US MMFs, and now tax reform.]

> I mention this in passing, but in countries that started off with a very bad fiscal situation [Luke: The US has the worst double deficit in the world], there is a lot of history that indicates that a slowdown, when a country faces a very bad fiscal situation, leads to still more recourse to the central bank and traders, seeing the writing on the wall that central bank financing will eventually lead to inflation. Everybody says: 'I am out of here.' There is a currency collapse and hyperinflation. We have seen it many times in history in the worst of the worst-case scenarios.

Luke: With all due respect, Mr. X, people are going to think you're crazy. Investors would never say "We are out of here" on the USD. The US could never suffer broad hyperinflation.

Mr. X: Oh, I agree that the US could never have broad hyperinflation, but I do think the USD could "hyperinflate" v. gold. I also think the US could see continued asset price inflation. In my view, broad hyperinflation in the US is highly unlikely because at the right price of everything, the US could be nearly self-sufficient in just about anything. Your shale sector has proven that beyond a doubt when the USD "collapsed" versus oil prices from 2003-2008, when oil ran from $20 to $147 per barrel, no?

However, you are missing the forest for the trees with your first point. The pronounced breakout of SPX v. TLT on a twenty-five-year chart strongly suggests *investors began saying "We are out of here" on the USD in 3q16*. [He passed me the following chart.]

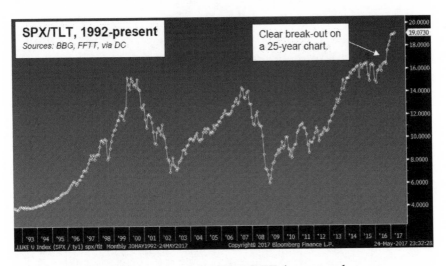

Mr. X: Investor flight out of the TLT ETF (twenty-plus-year USTs) and into SPX (big cap US equities whose revenues and earnings will rise significantly with a significant devaluation of the USD) has continued into 2018, as the average stock as represented by the Value Line Geometric Index just broke out above a twenty-year resistance level (as this chart from my friend Ben Woodward, a long-time money manager, shows). [He passed me another chart to illustrate his point.]

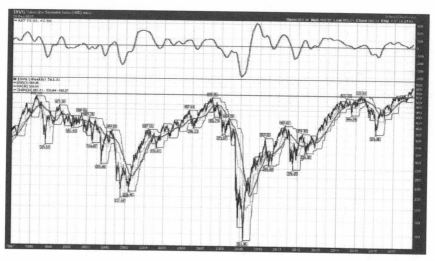

Luke: Oh, my God…I get it. We wrote about this exact thing last March, when we noted that if we adjusted the "Warren Buffett metric" (Equity Market Cap as a percentage of GDP) for the US Federal debt outstanding (that would have to eventually be monetized), we came to the conclusion that US equity markets were actually cheap! [It was now my turn to show Mr. X the following chart, which was accurate as of 3/30/17.]

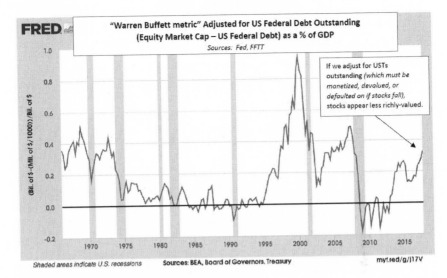

Mr. X: Correct. You absolutely get it.

Luke: So, your point is that once US tax receipts "tapped out" in the third quarter of 2016 from the "choking out" delivered by China and other global Central Banks beginning in the third quarter of 2014, it became *fait accompli* that the US would see "asset hyperinflation" as traders began to realize the only option left was "Option #4, significant USD devaluation."

Mr. X: Yes, that is exactly my point, and Mr. Market seems to have begun discounting it back in the third quarter of 2016, and is more aggressively discounting it as we speak.

Luke: Wow. Massive implications. Why don't we stop there. We've given readers a lot to think about. Thank you again for your time.

Mr. X: You bet. Thank you for the discussion!

Chapter 3

WHY THE US MAY "BURN DOWN THE WORLD"

TO DEFEND THE USD

MAY 2018

Four months after I met with Mr. X in Chicago, he was back in New York, so I flew there to meet him. As we sat down to dinner, Mr. X looked grim.

Luke: Mr. X, it is great to see you again.

Mr. X: It's great to see you too, Luke.

Luke: Let me start out by asking you about the hottest topic of the day: What's your take on the recent bounce of the USD?

Mr. X: I think the perception of a more hawkish Fed has driven a bit of a bounce in the USD that could continue for a bit, but ultimately, what the BIS [Bank for International Settlements] said eighteen months ago was true then, and it is still true now.

Luke: For the benefit of our readers, can you remind us what the BIS said?

Mr. X: Sure. In a white paper published in late 2016, the BIS, the Central Bankers' Central Bank, was quite clear. It said, "There may be no winners from a stronger USD." [Mr. X then read to me from the following article, emphasizing the key points he wanted me to understand.]

> Could it be that the tighter financial conditions resulting from the stronger dollar have been a drag on export growth? More work is needed here but this is an issue of first-order importance…
>
> What is new is that the bank/capital markets nexus has gone global. *The VIX was the barometer of deleveraging pressures in 2008, but now it is the dollar.*
>
> In this respect, the three great economic puzzles of our time—slow productivity growth, the slowdown in trade, and the failure of covered interest parity—may all be related. Given the dollar's role as a barometer of global appetite for leverage, *there may be no winners from a stronger dollar.*
>
> **Bank/Capital Markets Nexus goes global – BIS, 11/15/16**
>
> http://www.bis.org/speeches/sp161115.pdf

Luke: I remember that BIS white paper well; it came right after Donald Trump was elected, and at a time when markets were betting heavily on a stronger USD, which, of course, never came to pass; instead, the USD unexpectedly fell approximately 10 percent in 2017. Of course, of late, the USD has bounced in response to the perception of a more hawkish Fed, and it is now breaching critical technical levels against EM FX indices among other things.

Mr. X: Yes, it is. Whether it is this chart from our friend Raoul Pal over at Global Macro Investor (He handed me the chart on the next page)…

...or this chart [He pointed to the chart below] of EUR + JPY aggregate cross-currency basis swaps from our friend DC, suggesting a notable uptick in EU and Japanese demand for USDs since late 2017, it seems as if a number of important technical indicators are suggesting the Fed's more hawkish tone in recent months is having the desired effect on the USD.

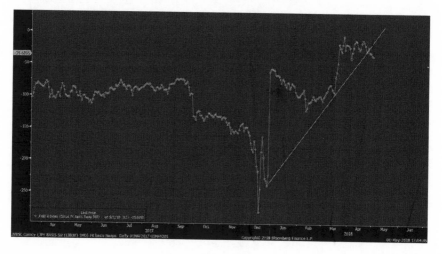

Luke: So, what do you make of this at least partially Fed-driven USD strength?

Mr. X: I would revisit your writings of October 2016, shortly before the US surprisingly elected President Trump; let me refresh your memory.... Here's what you wrote on page 2 of the marketing slide deck you gave me during our meeting then. [He read the following document to me.]

What if...

...the sharp rise in LIBOR does not stop after MMF reform goes live on 10/14/16 because its rise since 3Q14 has actually been an important symptom of US Federal "crowding out" of the private sector?

...ACA, MMF Reform, and Bank HQLA Reforms are actually patchwork US government regulatory responses to US foreign official creditors ceasing to lend money to the US government?

...after two years of pushing entitlement costs onto US consumers via ACA, the government's efforts to reduce US Federal deficits as a percentage of GDP are now instead *widening* US Federal deficits?

...the Fed's on-again, off-again rate hike discussions have nothing to do with the state of the US economy and everything to do with keeping the private sector funding US government deficits since the foreign official sector stopped doing so in 3Q14 (when global FX reserves peaked)?

...there is no massive US "Fiscal Stimulus" program coming because the US government already cannot afford the massive "Fiscal Stimulus" programs promised by the FDR and LBJ

Administrations (Social Security, Medicare/Medicaid)?

...there is no OPEC oil production freeze coming because the way the world is pricing oil has changed back to the way oil was priced from 1860-1973? (Free Market Oil System).

The market is currently trading as if none of these "What Ifs" will ever prove true. What if one of them did prove true? *What if all of them do?*

Mr. X: I would say your "What If" list above generally aged fairly well, no?

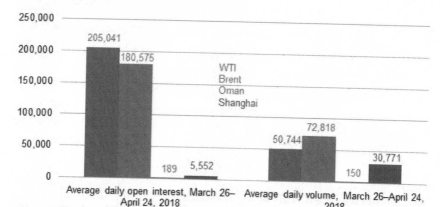

Figure 3. Trading data for various crude oil futures contracts for September 2018 delivery
number of contracts

Average daily open interest, March 26–April 24, 2018   Average daily volume, March 26–April 24, 2018

Source: CME Group, Intercontinental Exchange, Dubai Mercantile Exchange, Shanghai International Energy Exchange, Bloomberg, L.P.
Note: Because the Shanghai International Energy Exchange counts both long and short sides of a transaction, Shanghai's open interest and volume are halved to compare with the others.

Luke: Well, except for the last point about "No OPEC freeze"....

Mr. X: Yes, but you adjusted well, if I remember correctly, and perhaps more importantly, your broader point about the way the world is pricing oil changing has seemed to be completely on-point. [He handed me the following article.]

New Chinese crude oil futures contract could become Asian price benchmark – EIA, 4/25/18

https://www.eia.gov/petroleum/weekly/archive/2018/18042 5/includes/analysis_print.php

After one month of trading, the Shanghai futures contract for September 2018 delivery already has more open interest and trading volume than the Oman contract for September delivery. The Shanghai futures contract's open interest is smaller than that for Brent and WTI, but trading volume has been high compared with the number of contracts outstanding, indicating a high amount of trading turnover (Figure 3).

Luke: Well, thank you…and yes, I agree that the broader point about the way the oil is being priced globally has indeed begun changing more rapidly. However, I guess I'm left wondering why you brought up that list from our October 2016 slide deck in the context of a more hawkish Fed driving a stronger USD?

Mr. X: I bring it up because of the conclusion you made in that slide deck about the potential implications of your list above. Do you remember your list of potential implications?

Luke: Yes, I do, but again for the benefit of readers, will you rehash it?

Mr. X: Of course. Toward the end of that deck, on a slide entitled "What Does This Mean for 2H16 Macro Strategy?", you noted the following. [He read to me from a photocopy of the slide he had.]

"…the 2nd Oil Crisis could be worked through, slowly, but the international financial system could not survive a 3rd Oil Crisis—the inflation would make it impossible to recycle the petrodollars to the oil importing countries with any hope of repayment, trade would crumble, and the system would be brought to its knees." — BIS Chair Jelle Zijlstra, 1980

The world has now stopped recycling petrodollars to the oil importing countries, which implies one of three things:

1. The Fed must raise rates to drive foreign capital into USTs (or crash global markets trying to do so, which would also force a "safety-bid" for USTs/USDs, thereby funding the US government (if for only a brief time);

2. The US government must accelerate its efforts in forcing banks, pensions, and MMFs to buy USTs while also pushing even more entitlement costs onto US citizens via ACA, etc.;

3. The Fed must renew QE in amounts big enough to fund the US government ($100B+/month or more possibly), or otherwise devalue the USD.

Given options 1-3 above, we are surprised how few on Wall Street even seem to be considering the possibility that the Fed's rate hike discussions may have *nothing* to do with the US economy and *everything* to do with a last-ditch effort by the Fed to try to defend the USD, à la Paul Volcker 1979-1981 (which was obviously not a good time for risk assets).

If Wall Street conventional wisdom does not see the developing US government funding crisis, it cannot possibly consider that the Fed may be hiking rates to defend the USD. Conventional wisdom may be making a grave error—caveat emptor.

Shortly thereafter, you added a couple of other potential options to the list above—slashing government spending, or going to war with China and/or Russia to defend the USD—but in my opinion, your framework above is quite helpful in understanding why the Fed has become more hawkish, driving the USD higher, despite the BIS having noted eighteen months ago that "there may be no winners from a stronger USD."

Luke: Why do you think our framework above is helpful in understanding why the Fed might be working to strengthen the USD despite the pronouncement from the BIS that essentially said "a stronger USD is in nobody's interest"?

Mr. X: Because I would amend the BIS' statement slightly to say that a stronger USD is in *almost* nobody's interest. The US government needs the USD to remain the world's reserve currency in order to have a chance of keeping US Federal deficits sustainable. A stronger USD is very much in certain US government near-term interests.

Luke: Agreed...but I'm not sure I understand the point you're trying to make.

Mr. X: My point is that I think your analysis was dead-on, and shortly after President Trump got elected, he and his administration began jawboning the USD lower. In total, the USD fell nearly 10 percent last year. While I would not call that a "devaluation" in the classic sense of the term, as you noted in option 3 in your marketing deck from fall 2016, it certainly was a reduction in the value of the USD in 2017, a reduction in the USD's value that relieved some of the stresses in the system that you noted. In other words, the reduction in the USD's value in 2017 bought time.

Luke: Okay, I understand now. But I'm still not sure how this relates to the USD's bounce higher of late on the back of perceived increased Fed hawkishness.

Mr. X: I think the "playbook" you highlighted in your October 2016 slide deck is still valid, and the US has shifted its strategy from option #3 (weaken the USD), back to a combination of options #1 and #2. Let me read again from your marketing deck:

1. The Fed must raise rates to drive foreign capital into USTs (or crash global markets trying to do so, which would also force a "safety-bid" for USTs/USDs, thereby funding the US government (if for only a brief time).

2. The US government must accelerate its efforts in forcing banks, pensions, and MMFs to buy USTs while also pushing even more entitlement costs onto US citizens via ACA, etc.

In my eyes, the Fed has gotten more hawkish to try to defend the USD and drive more capital into USTs (particularly at the long end of the UST curve), while simultaneously implementing "Tax Reform" that appears to be merely the latest machination designed to drive capital into the US and into USTs. As you have noted, LIBOR has certainly reacted as it did during MMF Reforms and bank HQLA regulations (as have LIBOR/OIS spreads, not shown):

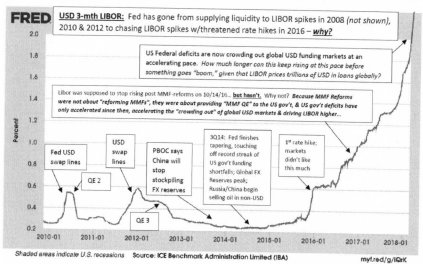

Shaded areas indicate U.S. recessions   Source: ICE Benchmark Administration Limited (IBA)   myf.red/g/IQrK

Luke: I agree. My question is <u>why do you think the Fed</u> <u>strategy changed from #3 (weaken the USD)</u>, b<u>ack to options 1</u> & 2?

Mr. X: I think because both the Fed and the US government have been quite spooked by recent events.

Luke: What events?

Mr. X: I would say there are two separate, acute sets of events that spooked the Federal Reserve, and one rapidly-accelerating development that spooked the US government.

Luke: Let's start with the Fed. What do you think has spooked them?

Mr. X: I think two major factors spooked the Fed. First, that the long end of the UST curve sold off in February's equity market sell-off, one of the fastest 10 percent equity market sell-offs in history. You can see it in the following series of charts…. Prior 10 percent equity market sell-offs post-2008 had always resulted in a bid for long-dated USTs (yields down), but in February 2018, investors did not flock into long-dated USTs, which sold off with stocks. This was highly unusual and can be seen in these charts. (Mr. X handed me a piece of paper with the following charts.]

Apr-10 thru Aug-10: SPX (in blue) down, 10y UST yields down.

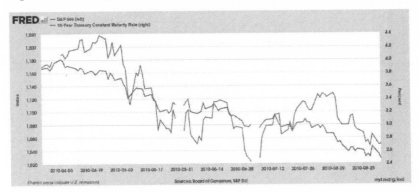

Aug 17, 2015 thru Aug 24, 2015: SPX (in blue) down, 10y UST yields down.

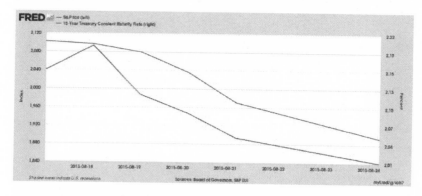

Jan 26, 2018 – Feb 8, 2018: SPX (in blue) down, *10y UST yields...up.*

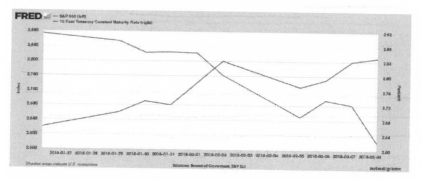

Luke: You think the Fed became fearful that it was beginning to lose control of the long end of the UST curve?

Mr. X: I think it understood that when you have an equity market sell-off and both your currency falls and your sovereign debt yields rise, that is not a good thing.

Luke: Agreed...that's Emerging Market funding issue-type market action.

Mr. X: Correct. Not something seen in the US very often.

Luke: No, it is not. You mentioned a second event that might have spooked the Fed into becoming more hawkish. What was that?

Mr. X: It's a corollary to UST yields rising in the February sell-off—Chinese government bonds were actually bid in the February market sell-off, even as USTs were sold. [He handed me the chart below.]

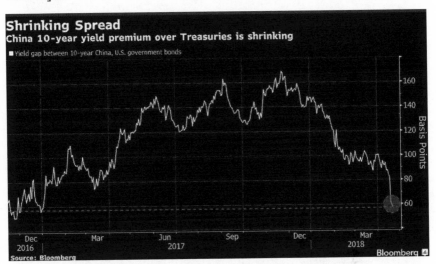

Shrinking Spread
China 10-year yield premium over Treasuries is shrinking
■ Yield gap between 10-year China, U.S. government bonds

Source: Bloomberg

Luke: Wow! Were there any technical factors that drove that?

Mr. X: Yes, apparently Chinese government bonds (CGBs) were recently approved to be added to a major EM bond index, which may have driven some front-running by funds beginning to build up their CGB holdings. While some have been dismissive of the yield convergence between CGBs & USTs for this reason, to me, such dismissiveness may be missing the forest for the trees.

Luke: Because…?

Mr. X: Because CGBs are being added to the global bond indices for a reason, likely due in no small part to increased global comfort with the CNY after its inclusion in the SDR eighteen months ago. Either way, CGBs are still becoming more relevant to the global financial system, apparently at the expense of USTs at some level (given the convergence above).

Luke: Gotcha; makes sense. You also mentioned that you thought some events may have spooked the US government. What are those?

Mr. X: This is just my opinion, of course, but my sense from watching geopolitical events, plus recent US geopolitical and trade actions, along with the sudden rapid vilification of China in the US and Western prestige media suggests to me that there may be a dawning realization by Western policymakers and assorted other Western establishment elites that not only is China playing by a different set of rules than the West, but the natural outcome of the collision of "China's rules" and "Western rules" is not a happy outcome for Western power on a relative basis. This is real *Game of Thrones*-type stuff.

Luke: What types of things have you seen that have led you to this conclusion?

Mr. X: Well, some of them you touched on in the 3/15/18 edition of FFTT. You (quite rightly in my opinion) noted there has been a pronounced shift in Western prestige media's attitude toward China as typified by some of these articles. [He passed to me the following excerpts of articles I had referenced.]

Washington strikes back against Chinese investment – *Foreign Policy Journal*, 3/6/18

https://foreignpolicy.com/2018/03/06/washington-strikes-back-against-chinese-investment/

> "The economics are clear: We should open the doors as wide as possible to foreign investment," says Smart. "The politics are far murkier when dealing with an actor as large and ambitious as

China, and when dealing with Chinese investors who may have a political agenda."

We got China wrong—now what? *Washington Post* – 2/28/18

https://www.washingtonpost.com/opinions/we-got-china-wrong-now-what/2018/02/28/39e61c0e-1caa-11e8-ae5a-16e60e4605f3_story.html?tid=ss_tw-amp

Remember how American engagement with China was going to make that communist backwater more like the democratic, capitalist West?

For years, both Republican and Democratic administrations argued that the gravitational pull of U.S.-dominated international institutions, trade flows, even pop culture, would gradually reshape the People's Republic, resulting in a moderate new China with which the United States and its Asian allies could comfortably coexist.

Well, Chinese President Xi Jinping has just engineered his potential elevation to president for life. This is the latest proof—along with China's rampant theft of U.S. intellectual property, its military buildup in the South China Sea and Xi's touting of Chinese-style illiberal state capitalism as "a new option for other countries"—that the powers-that-be in Beijing have their own agenda, impervious to U.S. influence.

The United States needs a long, sober policy rethink. Step one: Remember that friendlier ties with Beijing seemed like a good idea, even a brilliant one, when then-likely presidential candidate Richard M. Nixon first proposed it during the Cold War, also in the pages of *Foreign Affairs*, half a century ago.

Now it's evident China has been gaining leverage over the political and economic leaders of the United States and has learned how to make them defer to its norms.

If there's one clear lesson from the past 50 years of U.S. policy toward China, it's that nothing is inevitable in international politics, or irreversible. From now on, the United States must act accordingly.

The China Reckoning: How Beijing Defied American Expectations – 2/13/18

https://www.foreignaffairs.com/articles/united-states/2018-02-13/china-reckoning

Even those in U.S. policy circles who were skeptical of China's intentions still shared the underlying belief that U.S. power and hegemony could readily mold China to the United States' liking.

Nearly half a century since Nixon's first steps toward rapprochement, the record is increasingly clear that Washington once again put too much faith in its power to shape China's trajectory. All sides of the policy debate erred: free traders and financiers who foresaw inevitable and increasing openness in China, integrationists who argued that Beijing's ambitions would be tamed by greater interaction with the international community, and hawks who believed that China's power would be abated....

Mr. X: Leading up to the prior articles, I watched as several different senior US government officials explicitly threatened China, and more recently vocalized outright fear of China's plans:

Mnuchin threatens banning China from "dollar system" (SWIFT) – 9/12/17

https://www.bloomberg.com/news/articles/2017-09-12/mnuchin-threatens-financial-sanctions-on-china-over-north-korea

Trump to accuse China of 'economic aggression': FT – 12/17/17

https://www.ft.com/content/1801d4f4-e201-11e7-8f9f-de1c2175f5ce

> HR McMaster, US national security adviser who oversaw the strategy, this week said China—along with Russia—was a "revisionist power" that was "undermining the international order."

US to decide on trade sanctions against China this month – 1/10/18

https://asia.nikkei.com/Politics-Economy/International-Relations/US-to-decide-on-trade-sanctions-against-China-this-month

US Commerce Secretary Ross calls China 2025 plan "frightening" – 4/24/18

https://www.msn.com/en-us/money/markets/us-commerce-secretary-calls-china-2025-plan-frightening/ar-AAwiivL?ocid=spartanntp

Luke: Why do you think the tone on China changed the way it has, and changed so rapidly? What "international order" is "revisionist power" China undermining?

Mr. X: The international order that has the USD-centric system at the center of it, with US officials, therefore, in control of it.

Luke: Some would say that sounds like conspiracy-theory stuff. How is China violating those rules?

Mr. X: By using the flaws of the USD-centric system against itself.

Luke: How are they doing that?

Mr. X: The core underlying mechanics of the USD-centric system are pretty straightforward—the world exports goods to the US, the US exports USDs back to the world, and the world then finances US government deficits by recycling those USDs into USTs, US Agency securities, and the US financial system more broadly.

Luke: Okay, I understand that, so what is China doing in contravention to those "USD-centric system" rules?

Mr. X: They stopped buying USTs five years ago (after openly announcing they would stop buying USTs, per below):

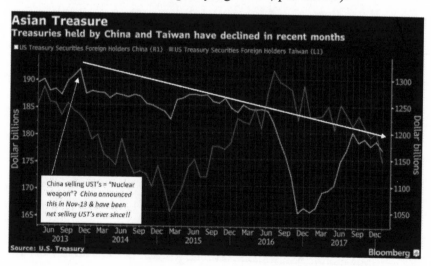

Asian Treasure
Treasuries held by China and Taiwan have declined in recent months

■ US Treasury Securities Foreign Holders China (R1)   ■ US Treasury Securities Foreign Holders Taiwan (L1)

China selling UST's = "Nuclear weapon"? *China announced this in Nov-13 & have been net selling UST's ever since!!*

Source: U.S. Treasury

Bloomberg

PBOC says no longer in China's favor to boost record FX reserves (i.e. UST holdings) – 11/23/18
https://www.bloomberg.com/news/articles/2013-11-20/pboc-says-no-longer-in-china-s-favor-to-boost-record-reserves

Luke: I can't say I blame them. It seems clear that given US Entitlement obligations, there's no possible way the US can make good on the $100T+ it owes in debt and entitlements on a real basis. But if that's the case, if China's not funding US deficits anymore as they are supposed to according to the "USD-centric international order," what are they buying with the USDs they earn from trade?

Mr. X: They've been acting very deliberately and methodically to "undermine" the "USD-centric international order." The first step they've taken is buying stakes in real assets and companies all over the world. Just Google "China invest or China buying" and read. Alibaba's Jack Ma also recently explicitly stated what China is doing. [He handed me the following article.]

Alibaba's Jack Ma: "Countries need to break free of US dominance of the semiconductor industry" – 4/25/18

http://m.scmp.com/tech/china-tech/article/2143352/countries-need-break-free-us-dominance-semiconductor-industry?amp=1&__twitter_impression=true

Mr. X: By their actions of buying up assets all over the world, China is essentially saying "You keep the USDs. We'll keep the chemicals, energy, property, mining, software IP, etc. assets." This is *not* how it's supposed to go according to the "USD-centric international order." However, this has been going on for years. Therefore, it is the more recent second step in the process that is, in my opinion, the more unforgivable sin by China.

Luke: What is this second step that is the "more unforgivable sin" by China?

Mr. X: China is not only exchanging USDs for control of physical assets all over the world, but it is now moving to price those assets in its own currency, in plain sight for even the most willfully-blind US policymaker to see. [Mr. X handed me the following articles.]

China oil futures launch may threaten primacy of USD: UBS – 3/26/18

https://www.reuters.com/article/us-china-oil-futures-dollar/china-oil-futures-launch-may-threaten-primacy-of-u-s-dollar-ubs-idUSKBN1H227E

> Already on Monday, Unipec, the trading arm of Asia's largest refiner Sinopec, has inked a deal with a western oil major to buy Middle East crude priced against the newly-launched Shanghai crude futures contract.

China taking first steps to pay for oil in CNY this year: sources – 3/29/18

https://www.reuters.com/article/us-china-oil-yuan-exclusive/exclusive-china-taking-first-steps-to-pay-for-oil-in-yuan-this-year-sources-idUSKBN1H51FA

> Shifting just part of global oil trade into the yuan is potentially huge. Oil is the world's most traded commodity, with an annual trade value of around $14 trillion, roughly equivalent to China's gross domestic product last year.

> A pilot program for yuan payment could be launched as early as the second half of this year, two of the people said.

Regulators have informally asked a handful of financial institutions to prepare for pricing China's crude imports in the yuan, said the three sources at some of the financial firms.

"Being the biggest buyer of oil, it's only natural for China to push for the usage of yuan for payment settlement. This will also improve the yuan liquidity in the global market," said one of the people briefed on the matter by Chinese authorities.

Under the plan being discussed, Beijing could possibly start with purchases from Russia and Angola, one of the people said, although the source had no details of anything in the works.

If successful, it could also trigger shifting other product payments to CNY, including metals and mining raw materials.

PBOC improves cross-border CNY payment system CIPS, to now operate 24 hours/day up from 12 hours – 5/2/18

https://www.wsj.com/articles/pboc-makes-improvements-to-cross-border-yuan-payment-system-1525251799?mod=e2twcb

Russia increases grip on Chinese oil market by opening 2nd ESPO pipeline doubling capacity to 600k bpd – 1/1/18

https://www.bloomberg.com/news/articles/2018-01-01/second-chinese-crude-oil-pipeline-linked-to-russia-s-espo-opens

Iran exports 784k bpd of oil to China in September, up 59% y/y [Luke: All in CNY] – 10/25/17

http://www.presstv.com/Detail/2017/10/25/539830/Irans-oil-exports-to-China-up-59

Saudis may seek funding in CNY – 8/24/17

https://www.reuters.com/article/us-saudi-china/saudis-may-seek-funding-in-chinese-yuan-idUSKCN1B413R

Luke: Oh, my gosh, it is pretty obvious when you put it like that….

Mr. X: It really is, isn't it?

Luke: Why doesn't the US do something about it?

Mr. X: What is the US going to do—tell China and, therefore, the world that USDs are not good for anything but USTs? If they did that, the US would all but apply the *coup de grace* to the USD's reserve status themselves, especially now that the CNY infrastructure above is nearly in place and China controls such a large amount of physical commodities and assets all over the world because Westerners were so willing to exchange them for USDs…the same USDs the US must emit $100T or more of in coming decades unless the US government is to default on either its external or internal commitments (USTs or entitlements.)

Luke: Can't we sanction the nations supporting CNY oil and commodity pricing—Russia, China, Iran, or…never mind. We already are, aren't we?

Mr. X: Indeed. Want to know something else that's really incredible about all of this?

Luke: What?

Mr. X: Chinese military hardliners were calling for China to do this to the US in 1999, as the US advocated that China be allowed into the WTO and a full two years before China joined the WTO!

[Mr. X read to me the following, again emphasizing the key points.]

Chinese general says contain the US by attacking its finances – 2/16/16

https://www.theepochtimes.com/chinese-general-says-contain-the-united-states-by-attacking-its-finances_1967150.html

> *To effectively contain the United States, other countries shall think more about how to cut off the capital flow to the United States while formulating their strategies,"* writes Maj. Gen. Qiao Liang, a professor at the People's Liberation Army (PLA) National Defense University, in an op-ed published in China Military Online, the official mouthpiece of the PLA. *"That's the way to control America's lifeblood."*
>
> Qiao is one of the leading voices on China's uses of economic warfare and its broader military strategies using unconventional warfare. *In 1999, when Qiao was still a colonel, he co-authored the book "Unrestricted Warfare" with another colonel, Wang Xiangsui.*
>
> *In "Unrestricted Warfare" Qiao and Wang promoted the use of terrorism, cyberattacks, legal warfare (also called "lawfare"), and economic warfare against the United States.* While "Unrestricted Warfare" was published 17 years ago, many of the strategies it proposed can now be seen playing out.

Luke: My goodness….

Mr. X: I know, right? It gets better. Take a read of this. [He handed me a printed sheet.]

China increases its gold reserves in order to kill two birds with one stone

The China Radio International sponsored newspaper *World News Journal* (Shijie Xinwenbao) (04/28/11): "According to China's National Foreign Exchanges Administration China's gold reserves have recently increased. Currently, the majority of its gold reserves have been located in the U.S. and European countries.

The U.S. and Europe have always suppressed the rising price of gold. They intend to weaken gold's function as an international reserve currency. They don't want to see other countries turning to gold reserves instead of the U.S. dollar or Euro. Therefore, suppressing the price of gold is very beneficial for the U.S. in maintaining the U.S. dollar's role as the international reserve currency.

China's increased gold reserves will thus act as a model and lead other countries towards reserving more gold. Large gold reserves are also beneficial in promoting the internationalization of the RMB."

> Wikileaks, 2011, Unclassified cable from US Beijing Embassy: http://cables.mrkva.eu/cable.php?id=204405

Luke: Wow....

Mr. X: The aforementioned Chinese general was even more explicit in 2015:

The most important event of the 20th century was the decoupling of the dollar from gold on August 15, 1971.

Since then, mankind has really seen the emergence of a financial empire that has brought the entire human race to its financial system. Actually, the so-called establishment of dollar hegemony started from this moment. Today, about 40 years time. And from this day on, we entered a real era of paper money, no precious metal behind the dollar, it fully supported by the government's credit and profited the world over.

To put it simply: Americans can get physical wealth from all over the world by printing a piece of green paper. There has never been such a thing in human history. In the history of mankind, there are many ways of getting wealth, either by currency exchange, by either gold or silver, or by war, but the cost of the war is enormous. When the dollar turns into a green paper, the cost of making profits in the United States can be extremely low.

By using this method, money is born by the Americans and then exported overseas. As a result, the United States turns itself into a financial empire. The United States has brought the entire world into its financial system.

Many people think that after the decline of the British Empire, the colonial history has basically come to an end. In actual fact, after the United States became a financial empire, it began to implicitly colonize and expand the United States dollar, so that the United States covertly controls the economies of all countries and turns all the countries in the world into its financial colony.

Today we see a lot of sovereign and independent countries, including China, *you can have sovereignty, a constitution, a government, but you are [never] separated from the dollar.* Everything you end up in various ways is expressed in U.S. dollars and eventually. *Your real wealth enters the*

71

United States through endless exchanges with the U.S. dollar.

It can only make money for its own money by allowing international capital to enter the financial pools of the major cities. Then, with the money they earn to cut wool all over the world, Americans are the only living law now. Or what we call in China the American way of living.

In this way, the United States needs a large capital return to support the daily life of the Americans and the U.S. economy. Under such circumstances, [any nation that] blocks the return of capital to the United States is the enemy of the United States. We must understand this matter clearly.

Source:
http://www.chuban.cc/dshd/jqjt/201504/t20150415_165579.html – translated, 4/15/15

Mr. X: Did you catch that part there at the end? "The US needs a large capital return to support the daily life of the Americans and the US economy. Under such circumstances, [any nation that] blocks the return of capital to the US is the enemy of the US. We must understand this matter clearly." Now, what did I just show you China began doing in 2013?

Luke: Blocking the return of capital to the US.

Mr. X: Exactly.

Luke: This does not seem to be a good scenario for EM or US risk assets for the balance of 2018.

Mr. X: I agree. My guess is we'll see tensions continue to rise, because China has clearly crossed a US redline, and the reasons China has done so are a redline for China—China cannot afford for its "Real wealth to enter the US through endless exchanges with the USD" as the Chinese general noted above; it will return to being a poor country if it does.

My guess is that the first step is likely continued escalation of trade tensions...but I am becoming increasingly fearful that the US is now deploying its "nuclear weapon of currency war."

Luke: Which is what?

Mr. X: The US Fed & Treasury will essentially weaponize the USD to an increasingly extreme degree, essentially destroying the global economy in order to preserve the USD's role as main reserve currency. If this option is chosen, the bet they are making is that it will drive demand for USDs and USTs higher, breaking global EM markets and commodities first, followed shortly thereafter by the US economy and, ultimately, the US fiscal situation.

Luke: Why would US authorities do such a thing if it will ultimately break the US economy and the US fiscal situation?

Mr. X: Because they believe they are less vulnerable than China and other EMs are to a rising USD and, therefore, the weaponization of the USD will not inflict as great a toll on the US' own economy before China and other EMs break. Let me think of a good metaphor for this.... Have you seen the Oliver Stone movie *Platoon*?

Luke: Yes, that is a tremendous and powerful movie.

Mr. X: To my eyes, the US may be engaging in the monetary equivalent of that movie's final scene, "calling in an airstrike inside their own wire" after they've been overrun, on the belief that collateral damage to some of their own "soldiers" is an acceptable outcome relative to the losses that would be suffered if the base were completely overrun.

Luke: If you're even directionally right, this is *not* a good outlook for risk assets of all stripes, starting with EMs and assets that look like EMs, such as commodities and including US shale producers, no? This is essentially what we have written about twice in the past month—the increasing risk of the Fed "shooting the hostage."

Mr. X: Yes, that is a good metaphor as well.

Luke: If the US deploys what you called "nuclear weapons of currency war" through the USD, does China have any countermeasures it can use?

Mr. X: Yes, it does. Recall that both former US Secretary of State Kerry and former US President Obama warned us in a ten-day time span in August 2015 how China might respond to any such threats. Obama said:

> We cannot dictate the foreign, economic and energy policies of every major power in the world. In order to even try to do that, we would have to sanction, for example, some of the world's largest banks. We'd have to cut off countries like China from the American financial system.
>
> And since they happen to be major purchasers of our debt, such actions could trigger severe disruptions in our own economy, and, by the way, raise questions internationally about the dollar's role as the world's reserve currency. That's part of the reason why many of the previous unilateral sanctions were waived.

Luke: How might China end the USD's reserve currency status as a "nuclear weapon of currency war"?

Mr. X: Remember from earlier that China is increasing gold reserves to "kill two birds with one stone." China understands gold is anathema to US authorities in particular, and as such, the establishment of a mechanism to settle offshore CNY balances in physical gold settlement in Shanghai, Hong Kong, and Dubai hints at how China, Russia, and others could use gold as a "nuclear weapon of currency war" of their own. As we have discussed before, it appears to my eyes that China has reopened a new "Bretton Woods gold window" at a floating price, through CNY.

In light of this, gold's refusal to sell-off with rising US real rates as it normally would is particularly interesting to me. [Mr. X handed me the chart below to illustrate his point.]

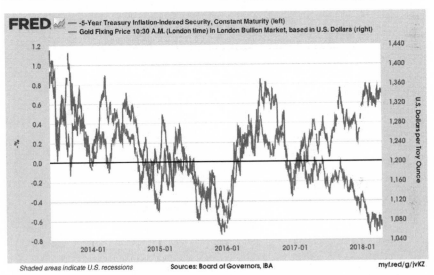

It suggests that perhaps some people understand gold may have an important role to play if currency wars further intensify, as it now appears they might; consequently, they are unwilling to sell gold as they normally would, given rising US real rates.

Luke: Do you think these risks are on anyone else's radar?

Mr. X: I think this risk is beginning to enter Wall Street's collective consciousness at an accelerating pace. Whether it is the

Wall Street Journal now openly acknowledging what China, Russia, and Iran are trying to do… [He handed me some articles and charts and pointed at them as he made his points.]

China, Iran seek to loosen USD's grip on global markets – 4/23/18

https://www.wsj.com/amp/articles/dollar-is-still-king-of-the-hill-globally-despite-other-nations-efforts-1524481200

…or Deutsche Bank beginning to write about US "Twin Deficits'" potential impact on the USD [chart on below]…

…or Bank of America noticing that USTs have begun trading like risky assets rather than the "safe haven par excellence" assets they have historically represented, noting:

> "Treasury performance has been akin to a risky asset. Our US rates team have highlighted numerous reasons for structural upward pressure on Treasury yields, including the Fed's balance sheet shrinkage, higher US Libor [sic] rates and importantly…the jump in the US budget deficit."
>
> — Bank of America Merrill Lynch's Barnaby Martin, April 2018

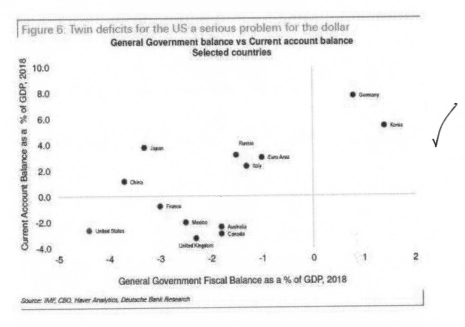

Figure 6: Twin deficits for the US a serious problem for the dollar
General Government balance vs Current account balance
Selected countries

Source: IMF, CBO, Haver Analytics, Deutsche Bank Research

Luke: Wow. If you're even directionally right, this has massive implications for global markets and economies, soon. Why don't we stop there. We've given readers a lot to think about. Thank you again for your time.

Mr. X: You bet. Thank you for the discussion!

Chapter 4

THE USAPPEARS TO BE FORCING THE EU INTO AN EXISTENTIAL CHOICE OVER THE NORD STREAM 2 PIPELINE

JUNE 7, 2018

Five weeks after we met in New York, Mr. X unexpectedly called me on my cell phone.

Mr. X: Luke, I'm on my way from Los Angeles to New York and thought I would stop in Cleveland—are you available for dinner tonight, on short notice?

Luke: I am.

Mr. X: Perfect. I'll tell my pilot to file a new flight plan that stops off in Cleveland. What's the best airport to use?

Luke: I would use either Burke Lakefront Airport or there is also a business jet center at Cleveland Hopkins Airport. Your pilot should know what is easiest. I can meet you either place and we'll go to dinner.

Mr. X: Perfect. I'll call you with our arrival time once our new flight plan is filed. See you soon.

About thirty minutes later, Mr. X called and told me he'd be
landing at Cleveland Hopkins; I drove to the business jet center
and picked him up. We made small talk on the way to a local
restaurant, catching up on each other's families and recent travel.
Then we settled into a quiet booth in the basement of a local pub
and got down to business.

**Luke: When I talked to you five weeks ago, I didn't anticipate
talking to you again so soon. To what do I owe the pleasure of
your visit?**

Mr. X: When we talked five weeks ago, I said that the US may be
engaging in the monetary equivalent of the final scene of Oliver
Stone's movie *Platoon*, metaphorically calling in an airstrike
inside their own wire after they've been overrun, on the belief that
collateral damage to some of their own "soldiers" is an acceptable
outcome relative to the losses that would be suffered if the base
were completely overrun.

**Luke: Indeed. I thought it was a terrific and apt metaphor. Do
you still think it an apt metaphor?**

Mr. X: Yes, and it appears to be happening faster than I expected.

**Luke: Is there a particular trigger for it happening sooner than
you expected?**

Mr. X: Yes. It appears that the Nord Stream 2 pipeline may be a
key trigger. [He passed to me the following two articles.]

> **Trump presses Germany to drop Russian pipeline as
> condition for avoiding a trade war – 5/17/18**
>
> https://www.wsj.com/articles/trump-presses-germany-to-
> drop-russian-pipeline-for-trade-deal-1526566415

Trump Forbids Russian Pipeline. Europe Pushes Back – 5/18/18

https://www.bloomberg.com/view/articles/2018-05-18/nord-stream-2-pipeline-is-new-front-in-u-s-clash-with-europe

> *The Wall Street Journal* reported Thursday that President Donald Trump is demanding that Germany drop Nord Stream 2 as one of the conditions of a trade deal with Europe that wouldn't include high tariffs on steel and aluminum.

> In addition to these conflicts, the U.S. has threatened sanctions on European companies involved with Nord Stream 2, including powerful multinationals such as Royal Dutch Shell, Austria's OMV, France's Engie and Germany's Uniper and Wintershall. Now, even EU officials and national leaders who have no particular love for Nord Stream 2 are on the side of Germany.

Luke: Weird. Why would the US care whether Germany buys gas from Russia?

Mr. X: Well, one reason seems sure: It is not because the US is concerned with the sanctity of free markets in this case. After all, per *The Wall Street Journal* article, Russian gas is "at least 20% cheaper" than competing US LNG:

> Liquefied gas from the U.S. needs to be shipped over the Atlantic and would be considerably more expensive than Russian gas delivered via pipelines. A senior EU official working on energy regulation said Russian gas would be at least 20% cheaper.

Source: https://www.wsj.com/articles/trump-presses-germany-to-drop-russian-pipeline-for-trade-deal-1526566415

Luke: Why does the US care about this pipeline so much now?

Mr. X: Perhaps because construction on the Nord Stream 2 pipeline is finally beginning, after numerous delays:

Nord Stream 2 is the 2nd phase of an existing pipeline that already channels [a] smaller amount of gas from Russia to Germany. Construction for the second phase started this week in Germany, after investors committed €5 billion to the venture.

Source: https://www.wsj.com/articles/trump-presses-germany-to-drop-russian-pipeline-for-trade-deal-1526566415

Luke: Let me rephrase my question: Why is the US government, which publicly says it supports free and fair markets, trying to force the EU to pay more than 20 percent more for gas, in effect trying to dictate EU energy policy?

Mr. X was smiling as he handed me the next article.

Mr. X: This might explain it.

"Subjects under the influence of power, he [Dacher Keltner, a psychology professor at UC Berkeley] found in studies spanning two decades, acted as if they had suffered a traumatic brain injury—becoming more impulsive, less risk-aware, and, crucially, less adept at seeing things from other people's point of view."

"Power Causes Brain Damage" – *The Atlantic*, August 2017

https://www.theatlantic.com/magazine/archive/2017/07/power-causes-brain-damage/528711/

Mr. X: It's interesting, isn't it? The world's poets long ago coined the phrase "drunk on power," and centuries later, here we have modern science confirming what the world's poets knew then— power makes one "drunk," or perhaps more aptly, "punch drunk."

Luke: Wow…that study would certainly explain a lot of the economic and geopolitical policy decisions of many of the world's nations, both recently and throughout history. However, I was trying to be more specific, so let me rephrase my question again: Why is the US government so opposed to this Russian/German pipeline?

Mr. X: Well, to understand that Luke, you must understand the broader context of US and UK foreign policy of the past 100-120 years and how that foreign policy has been heavily influenced by the writings of Sir Halford Mackinder.

Luke: Mackinder?

Mr. X: Yes. In 1919, Sir Halford Mackinder called Eurasia "the world-island" when he wrote: "Who rules East Europe commands the Heartland; who rules the Heartland commands the World-Island; who rules the World-Island commands the world."

More recently, in the 1950s, the UK's Lord Ismay famously said that NATO was created to "Keep the Soviet Union out, the Americans in, and the Germans down."

More recently still, Zbigniew Brzezinski laid it all out in his 1997 book *The Grand Chessboard*. [He handed me another printed piece of paper from Brzezinski's book.] Here, read this; it's all right there in black in white:

For America the chief prize is Eurasia…. About 75% of the world's people live in Eurasia, and most of the world's physical wealth is there as well, including about 75% of the world's known energy resources…. The Eurasian Balkans are infinitely more important as a potential economic prize: an enormous concentration of natural gas and oil reserves is located in the region, in addition to important minerals, including gold.

Potentially, the most dangerous scenario would be a grand coalition of China, Russia, and perhaps Iran, an 'anti-hegemonic' coalition united not by ideology but by complementary grievances. It would be reminiscent in scale and scope of the challenge posed by the Sino-Soviet bloc, though this time China would likely be the leader and Russia the follower. Averting this contingency, however remote it may be, will require a display of U.S. geostrategic skill on [all] perimeters of Eurasia simultaneously.

Mr. X: Most recently of all, just last week in fact, an anonymous EU official explicitly quoted Mackinder's theory in discussing the US' protestations regarding Nord Stream 2:

> We are risking all our energy resources over [the US'] Halford Mackinder geopolitical analysis that they must break up Russia and China.

> **Oil & gas geopolitics: No shelter from the storm – 5/31/18**

> http://www.atimes.com/article/oil-and-gas-geopolitics-no-shelter-from-the-storm/

Luke: Wow. It's all right there, isn't it? What long-time US policy titan Zbigniew Brzezinski called "the most dangerous scenario"—"a grand coalition of China, Russia, and perhaps

Iran"—would come to fruition if the Nord Stream 2 pipeline goes live, wouldn't it?

Russian gas pipelines would then be connecting China, Russia, and Europe, as well as potentially Iran. NATO's goal of "keeping the Soviet Union out, the US in and the Germans down" would have suffered a terminal blow.

Mr. X: Especially when the President of Russia explicitly and repeatedly said that the USD has no place in such a "grand coalition of China, Russia, and perhaps Iran." [He pulled out the next two articles and quoted from them, emphasizing the key points he wanted to make.]

Putin says USD monopoly in global energy trade is damaging economy – 8/14/14

https://uk.reuters.com/article/ukraine-crisis-putin-dollar/putin-says-russia-should-aim-to-sell-energy-in-roubles-idUKL6N0QK3BP20140814

> President Vladimir Putin said on Thursday Russia should aim to sell its oil and gas for roubles globally because *the dollar monopoly in energy trade was damaging Russia's economy.*
>
> "We should act carefully. At the moment we are trying to agree with some countries to trade in national currencies," Putin said during a visit to the Crimea region, which Moscow annexed from Ukraine earlier this year.

Putin: It's "quite possible" Russia could join EU currency zone, create currency that would eclipse the USD – 11/26/10

https://www.telegraph.co.uk/finance/currency/8163347/Putin-Russia-will-join-the-euro-one-day.html

> Can it be supposed that one day Russia will be in
> some joint currency zone with Europe? Yes, quite
> possible.... *We should move away from the*
> *excessive monopoly of the dollar as the only global*
> *reserve currency.*

**Luke: I have to give it to him—Putin has been very consistent
in his stance on the USD.**

Mr. X: (smiling) Perhaps his longstanding stance on the problems
the USD's monopoly in energy markets is causing has something
to do with how the US and the various USD-centric multi-lateral
institutions and officials feel about him, no? Interestingly, I have
had at least one senior Western Central Bank official confide to me
views very similar to those of Putin on the USD....

Luke: Wait, what? What'd they say?

Mr. X: That the core problem with the world's economic
imbalances is the USD, and more specifically, the USD-centric
system.

Luke: Yet they won't say that publicly?

Mr. X: Such things cannot be said publicly by "serious people"
until they are allowed to be said publicly, Luke. So let me return to
my timeline. Around the time China and Russia must have been
heavily negotiating over the terms of the Holy Grail deal, President
Obama said the following:

> **Obama: "Syria & Ukraine are not some Cold War
> chessboard" – 2/19/14**
>
> https://www.politico.com/story/2014/02/barack-obama-
> press-conference-russia-syria-ukraine-103707

**Luke: There's that word again, "chessboard." The same word
Brzezinski used in the title of his book.**

Mr. X: Correct. Perhaps Obama's choice of the word "chessboard" was not pure coincidence? [He passed me the following article to support his point.]

Brzezinski backs Sen. Obama – 8/25/07

http://www.washingtonpost.com/wp-dyn/content/article/2007/08/24/AR2007082402127.html

Mr. X: Of course, the reality is that despite Obama's protestations to the contrary in 2014, the US had already long been viewing EU energy politics through the lens of "some Cold War chessboard." Here's President George W. Bush's former Secretary of State, Condoleezza Rice, in 2014. [Mr. X proceeded to read the following transcript from the linked video; he later provided the link for me.]

> I'm quite an admirer of Chancellor Merkel, and I heard her statement when she was in Washington with President Obama, and I thought it was a very good statement, but now we need to have tougher sanctions, and I'm afraid that at some point this is probably going to have to involve oil and gas.
>
> The Russian economy is vulnerable. 80% of Russian exports are in oil, gas, and minerals. People say "well the Europeans will run out of energy." Well, the Russians will run out of cash before the Europeans run out of energy. And I understand that it is uncomfortable, to have an effect on business ties in this way, but this is one of the few instruments that we have.
>
> Over the long run, you simply want to change the structure of energy dependence, you want to depend more on the North American energy platform, the tremendous bounty of oil and gas that we are finding in North America. You want to have pipelines that don't go through Ukraine and Russia.

For years, we've been trying to get the Europeans interested in different pipeline routes. It's time to do that. And so some of this is simply acting, and acting as quickly as possible.

Former US Secretary of State Condoleezza Rice's interview on German television on energy, Russia - 5/16/14

https://youtu.be/aF0uYIjaTNE

Luke: But why does the US care about EU energy policies? The Cold War ended in 1989; we won.

Mr. X: Because this isn't about the Cold War or gas, Luke; it's about the US dollar, and specifically, its primary reserve status. ✓

Luke: Why do you say that?

Mr. X: (smiling and handing me a printed article) Because multiple former Washington establishment types who could talk plainly about it in 2014 were talking plainly about it. First came Charles Duelfer, who spent more than twenty-five years in the national security agencies of the US government, where he was involved in policy development, operations, and intelligence in the Middle East, Africa, Central America, and Asia:

> American media seems to be focused on domestic affairs while astonishing things are going on beyond the borders— and we seem to stand by watching helplessly. The United States position of prominence is eroding. Yesterday, at a summit in Shanghai between China's President Xi Jinping and Russian President Vladimir Putin a massive 30-year natural gas deal was signed to provide Russian gas to China. The agreement has been under negotiation for years and its fruition is a big deal for energy markets and international politics.

Less noticed, but possibly even more interesting, was an agreement between Russia and China aimed at undermining the role of the US dollar as the base currency. The Russian bank VTB and the Bank of China signed an agreement in the presence of Xi and Putin to avoid using the dollar and conduct exchanges in domestic currencies. This is a really big signal. The all mighty dollar may not always be all mighty.

Look at the world (or even just the United States) from the position of China. What makes America a super power? Is it the military? Partly. Is it nuclear weapons? Not so much. What really gives us leverage is the position of the dollar as the base currency. In the last financial crisis, we escaped largely by printing money. Other countries can't get away with that without causing massive inflation.

Sitting in Beijing, it could be seen as a financial attack— US Treasury printing tons on [sic] dollars that has the effect of exporting inflation to other countries. We borrow money (by selling treasuries to finance our wars, debt, TARP, etc.) and then pay them off by, in essence, printing dollars. The role of the dollar as base currency is a uniquely powerful lever. It is one that is rarely thought of in terms of national security, but nothing is more important. If we lose it, we will have lost our position as the last super power. Period.

Beijing, Moscow, and others are well aware of this. The role of the dollar also gives us the currently valuable tool of sanctions. If Washington decides to limit banking use of dollars for transactions with certain entities, e.g., in Russia or Iran, then we can impose our will on the international financial system. You can bet there is no higher strategic priority than to undermine that position. We are blindly squandering this leverage from inattention and by our inability to control our appetite for printed dollars. This is a national security issue, not just a budget issue.

American Vulnerability—The Dollar: Charles Duelfer - May 22, 2014

http://www.charlesduelfer.com/blog/?p=239

Mr. X now handed me a second printed article, a transcript from the video listed below.

Mr. X: Less than five months later, Lawrence Wilkerson, the former Chief of Staff to US Secretary of State Colin Powell, said something remarkably similar:

> What they want to do is use Putin and others' oil power, Petrodollars if you will, and I say that PetroYuan, PetroRenminbi, PetroEuro, whatever, to force the United States to lose its incredibly powerful role of owning the world's transactional action reserve currency.

> If that happens, a similar thing will happen to what Dwight Eisenhower threatened the British with, in the IMF, when they invaded Suez with the French and Israelis. The real powerful move that Ike made was to threaten a run on the [British] pound. Eden had to back off; he had to back off. He couldn't take that.

> So, what we're looking at is the possible use by others in the world of our dependence on the dollar to give us so much power that we otherwise would not have....Charles de Gaulle once said it was vicious what we did after the war when we had the world's reserve currency...and take that power away from us.

> And the [US Federal] debt increases enormously the capability [of these other nations] to do that. And the debt is staggering, if you think about it. If you just look at it and

understand what the Fed's been doing in terms of Quantitative Easing and just printing more and more money. The only reason you can do that is because you own the world's transactional reserve currency.

Lawrence Wilkerson, former Chief of Staff to US Secretary of State Colin Powell – October 8, 2014

https://www.youtube.com/watch?v=YM_MH_Bfq5c

Mr. X: It always catches my attention when multiple Washington policy veterans not in official positions (which means they can talk more openly than those still holding official positions) come out and say very similar things about events. These two certainly caught my attention.

Luke: Why do you think both of these gentlemen came out and talked about the pricing of oil and gas in non-USDs in such close proximity in 2014?

Mr. X: Mr. Duelfer told you. China and Russia signed the "Holy Grail" gas deal in May 2014. This deal was rumored to contain language that was cutting out the USD in energy transactions (something Putin had been vocally advocating for years for), and later on this was confirmed. [He handed me the following two articles.]

Russia signs 30-year "Holy Grail" gas deal with China – 5/21/14

https://www.bbc.com/news/business-27503017

Gazprom Neft sells all oil to China in renminbi rather than dollars – 6/1/15

https://www.ft.com/content/8e88d464-0870-11e5-85de-00144feabdc0

Gazprom Neft, the oil arm of state gas giant Gazprom, said on Friday that since the start of 2015 it had been selling in renminbi all of its oil for export down the East Siberia Pacific Ocean pipeline to China.

Luke: Interesting. Let me take a step back here and ask another bigger-picture question. All I hear in the US media is that Russia is a big threat to world peace and that the US needs to defend the EU against a potential Russian invasion. Isn't that true?

Mr. X: Let me answer your question with an observation. During the Cold War, a significant percentage of European gold reserves were held in either the US or UK to protect against those gold reserves being captured by the Soviets in case of a USSR invasion of Europe. It stands to reason then that if European Central Bankers still saw Russian invasion as a serious threat, they would keep their gold reserves safe and sound in the US and UK, no?

Luke: Makes sense.

Mr. X: So tell me, what should we infer from the fact that at least three major European Central Banks have repatriated substantial amounts of gold from the US and UK in the past four years, as testified to in these articles? [He handed me printed copies of the following articles.]

Dutch repatriates gold, becoming the latest EU country to address concerns about safety of its gold – 11/21/14

https://www.wsj.com/articles/dutch-repatriate-some-gold-reserves-1416568527

Germany repatriates gold stashed abroad during cold war – 8/23/17

https://www.ft.com/content/813c5460-87f9-11e7-bf50-e1c239b45787

Austria to repatriate some gold from UK – 5/28/15

https://www.reuters.com/article/austria-gold/austrian-central-bank-to-repatriate-some-gold-from-london-idUSV9N0VR01A20150528

Luke: That senior European Central Bank officials see little-to-no risk of any Russian invasion of Europe, that the mainstream US media may be overstating the risk.

Mr. X: Exactly. Watch what EU Central Banks do, Luke, not what the mainstream US media says. Want to know an interesting coincidence I noticed in the list above?

Luke: Sure!

Mr. X: Cross-check the list of EU Central Banks that have repatriated their gold from the US and UK with domicile against the list of EU energy companies being threatened with US sanctions for their participation in the Nord Stream 2 pipeline. We noted that the Dutch, the Germans, and the Austrians repatriated gold…. Now let's revisit which oil companies the US is threatening with sanctions. And *The Wall Street Journal* says:

> In addition to these conflicts, the U.S. has *threatened sanctions* on European companies involved with Nord Stream 2, including powerful multinationals such as *Royal Dutch Shell, Austria's OMV, France's Engie and Germany's Uniper and Wintershall.* Now, even EU officials and national leaders who have no particular love for Nord Stream 2 are on the side of Germany.

Trump Forbids Russian Pipeline. Europe Pushes Back – 5/18/18

https://www.bloomberg.com/view/articles/2018-05-18/nord-stream-2-pipeline-is-new-front-in-u-s-clash-with-europe

Luke: The Dutch, the Germans, and the Austrians.

Mr. X: Some coincidence, don't you think?

Luke: Indeed. Here's what I don't get: Let's say that Brzezinski's "Mackinderian most dangerous scenario" comes true, with Russian pipelines connecting Eurasia from coast-to-coast, with none of that energy transacting in USDs. It begs the question: What will that trade settle in? Neither China, the EU, nor Russia have a large sovereign bond market to recycle surpluses into, so this trade can never grow that large.

Mr. X: Well, Luke, the first answer is that the EU is a creditor region; Russia is a creditor nation; China is a creditor nation. What use would three of the world's biggest creditor nations have for a big sovereign debt market to settle imbalances? What imbalances? Imbalances will only be relatively minor, likely primarily around energy and commodity trade, no?

Even so, here too, there are some hints of what might actually be going on, if we're willing to put the pieces together and speculate a bit. Here's Charles Duelfer, from May 2014 again. Make sure to note the name of the Russian bank—VTB:

> The Russian bank VTB and the Bank of China signed an agreement in the presence of Xi and Putin to avoid using the dollar and conduct exchanges in domestic currencies. This is a really big signal. The almighty dollar may not always be almighty.

Now, here's gold analyst Koos Jansen, from October 2015…and note there's VTB Bank again:

Russia's VTB bank joins Shanghai Gold Exchange as member – 10/30/15

https://www.bullionstar.com/blogs/koos-jansen/strong-sge-withdrawals-chinese-gold-import/

> On the website of VTB Bank it was announced it has been granted SGE member status, with the right to participate in trading on the Shanghai International Gold Exchange (SGEI). VTB is the first Russian bank to enjoy member status of the Chinese exchange.
>
> "Access to trading on China's domestic precious metals market will give VTB Bank, which also trades on Western exchanges, more opportunities to sign gold deals in Shanghai. As an important element of our Chinese strategy, we continue working to develop the bank's business and that of our clients in the Shanghai Free Trade Zone…." said Herbert Moos, Chairman of VTB Bank's Management Board.
>
> The biggest part of Russia's mining output is sold to VTB and Sberbank, who sell it to the Russian central bank and foreign buyers—according to newswire EM Goldex.

Mr. X: Now, here we have an alternative media blog post of interest from November 2014 that I've shared with you before. [Mr. X read from the following article, emphasizing the key points for me again.]

Grandmaster Putin's Golden Trap – 11/23/14

https://www.gold-eagle.com/article/grandmaster-putins-golden-trap

Very few people understand what Putin is doing at the moment. And almost no one understands what he will do in the future. *No matter how strange it may seem, but right now, Putin is selling Russian oil and gas only for physical gold.*

Putin is not shouting about it all over the world. And of course, he still accepts US dollars as an intermediate means of payment. *But he immediately exchanges all these dollars obtained from the sale of oil and gas for physical gold!*

Not so long ago, British scientists have successfully come to the same conclusion, as was published in the Conclusion of the U.S. Geological survey a few years ago. Namely: Europe will not be able to survive without energy supply from Russia. Translated from English to any other language in the world it means: *"The world will not be able to survive if oil and gas from Russia is subtracted from the global balance of energy supply".*

Thus, the Western world, built on the hegemony of the petrodollar, is in a catastrophic situation. In which it cannot survive without oil and gas supplies from Russia. And Russia is now ready to sell its oil and gas to the West only in exchange for physical gold!

Luke: Look, I agree that's interesting, but I could dismiss that alternative media story as speculative.

Mr. X smiled and handed me another sheet of paper.

Mr. X: I thought you might say that. Yes, you're right; you could dismiss that story as speculative. However, you couldn't dismiss this chart. Remind me again—what is Russia's biggest export? Let's look at Condoleezza Rice's comments from 2014 again, shall we?

"80% of Russian exports are in oil, gas, and minerals."

Luke: Wow! Why is no one on Wall Street or in the US government saying anything about this?

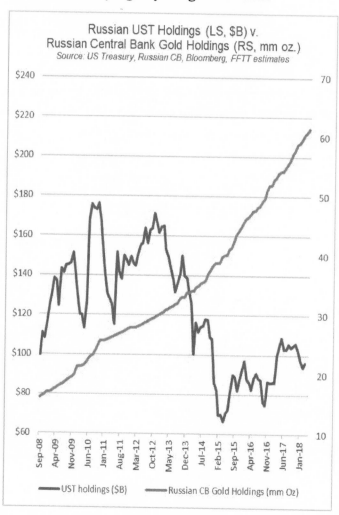

Mr. X: What are they going to do, announce the world's biggest energy exporter is settling trade in an asset the US government and Wall Street has spent the past forty years calling "useless"?

As Pulitzer-prize winning reporter Seymour Hersh said in discussing his new memoir:

> "To start with, it's important to understand many important stories are always hiding 'in the open.'"

Luke: So what do you expect to be the outcome of all of this?

Mr. X: I don't know. The US appears to be forcing the EU into an existential decision over the Nord Stream 2 pipeline: Will the EU be able to have sovereign power over EU energy policy (and, by extension, all of EU economic policy), or will the EU simply be an economic vassal of the US? I don't think many in the US understand that no less than that is at stake here.

Luke: I would agree with that. My sense is that heavy consensus among US investors is that the EU will just roll over; that the EU has no choice but to become the US' economic vassal. In fact, it is such a heavy consensus that I find myself wanting to take the other side, but I'm struggling for a reason to support such a contrarian view.

Mr. X: It's interesting you say that—I have been noticing a quiet groundswell lately of, shall we call it, discontent with the US' economic bullying, even among nations traditionally among the US' closest friends and allies. [Here Mr. X paused to laugh.] I mean, once even UK bankers begin referring to you as "You f*cking Americans," perhaps it's a sign your government has pressed its weaponization of the USD too far.

[He handed me the following articles to back up his point.]

US sanction power may be reaching its limit, "response to Iran decision shows global economy won't be bossed around forever" – 5/22/18

https://www.bloomberg.com/news/articles/2018-05-22/u-s-sanction-power-may-be-reaching-its-limit

> "You f***ing Americans," the message read. "Who are you to tell us, the rest of the world, that we're not going to deal with Iranians?" – UK banker, in 2012

EU to start Iran sanctions blocking law process to ban EU companies from complying w/US sanctions – 5/17/18

https://www.reuters.com/article/us-iran-nuclear-eu-response/eu-to-start-iran-sanctions-blocking-law-process-on-friday-idUSKCN1II20A

India says it only follows UN sanctions, not unilateral US sanctions on Iran – 5/28/18

https://www.reuters.com/article/us-india-iran/india-says-it-only-follows-un-sanctions-not-unilateral-us-sanctions-on-iran-idUSKCN1IT0WJ?feedType=RSS&feedName=worldNews

Australia & Japan still support the Iran deal – 5/9/18

https://www.apnews.com/7769da33651a449196128dbdf1bcf48c

Russia stands by Iran, condemns US sanctions – 5/23/18

http://www.xinhuanet.com/english/2018-05/23/c_137201107.htm

China will continue to cooperate w/Iran w/out violating int'l obligations, foreign ministry spokeswoman says – 6/4/18

https://www.pakistantoday.com.pk/2018/06/04/china-to-cooperate-with-iran-without-violating-international-obligations-fm/

Merkel Warns of G-7 Summit Split Over Trump's 'America First', says world becoming 're-ordered' globally – 6/6/18

https://www.bloomberg.com/news/articles/2018-06-06/merkel-warns-of-g-7-summit-split-over-trump-s-america-first

Mr. X: As we discussed before, President Obama warned in 2015 about the potential consequences of such a blowback.

Luke: Yes, we have always found it curious how both President Obama and Secretary of State Kerry linked Iranian sanctions to the USD's primary reserve status in a ten-day span in August 2015; it was almost as if they had both gotten the same talking points memo.

Mr. X: Yes, I remember you writing that. Here's the interesting thing—it almost seems as if the "USD primary reserve status at risk" talking points memo is being distributed more broadly these days.

Luke: What do you mean?

Mr. X: A topic that was once considered the strict purvey of "conspiracy theorists" is suddenly getting a lot of ink from "serious people." Remember my comment earlier that "Certain things are not allowed to be talked about until they are allowed to be talked about?" Perhaps we are at that point in this case, judging by how acceptable such talk has suddenly become. [Mr. X pulled out several articles and read the following excerpts from them.]

US sanction power may be reaching its limit, "response to Iran decision shows global economy won't be bossed around forever" – 5/22/18

https://www.bloomberg.com/news/articles/2018-05-22/u-s-sanction-power-may-be-reaching-its-limit

> "Europe & China have banks. One of these days, the US is going to talk the USD right out of its international role." – Jeff Sachs

The long arm of the USD—how to escape a hegemonic currency – May 2018

https://www.economist.com/finance-and-economics/2018/05/17/the-long-arm-of-the-dollar

> The more we condition use of the dollar and our financial system on adherence to US foreign policy, the more the risk of migration to other currencies and other financial systems...grows.

America beware: USD supremacy is not forever—under Trump, US increasingly seen as unreliable partner – 5/20/18

https://www.ft.com/content/3d4d1190-5931-11e8-806a-808d194ffb75

> China & South Korea are conducting trade using their own currencies rather than relying on the USD as a "vehicle currency". The logic for denominating in USD virtually all contracts for oil & other commodities is waning.

Donald Trump is jeopardizing the dollar's supremacy – 5/31/18

https://www.ft.com/content/7cc729c2-6328-11e8-a39d-4df188287fff?emailId=5b0f23ba9954000004bb6d9c

> The world could be entering an era of multiple reserve currencies, as Barry Eichengreen predicts. This has been typical through most of history. In between the world wars, the dollar and British pound shared the stage with the French franc and the Deutschemark. Today, the rival contenders would be the yuan & euro. The transition could even be a smooth one. But it is also possible that the US will have a massive debt shock, caused by a war, or another 2008-scale financial meltdown. A return to protectionism might do similar damage. At that point, the dollar would cease to be king.

"EU-US-Iran issue is existential for Swift as a global network": FT – 6/6/18

https://www.ft.com/content/9f082a96-63f4-11e8-90c2-9563a0613e56

> "Swift's very survival as a worldwide system for facilitating cross-border payments depends on it resisting such attempts to 'weaponize' it for political ends," said Nicolas Véron, senior fellow at the Peterson Institute for International Economics. "The Europe-US-Iran issue is existential for Swift as a global network," he said of the action against the company, which is owned by about 2,400 banks and other financial institutions.

Luke: Wow...the so-called "prestige financial media" is really warning about the US' actions, even as the EU, Australia,

Japan, India, China, Russia, and others are all warning the US they don't support unilateral sanctions.

Mr. X: Yes…it's almost like they're trying to establish a narrative. I will say, all of this reminds me of another instance of an immensely powerful nation taking one step too far. This instance happened much earlier in my life…but this setup makes me wonder if the US could be about to suffer its own "Suez Moment."

Luke: The US' own Suez Moment?

Mr. X: Sure—you can read more about the background of the UK's "Suez Moment" at your convenience here. [He pulled out yet another article.]

> https://defenceindepth.co/2016/11/16/the-significance-of-suez-1956-a-reference-point-and-turning-point/

But the punchline is here. [He read from the above article.]

> The military operation ended abruptly when the UN called for a cease-fire on 2 November. The conflict led to a run on the pound and a sudden decline in Britain's gold reserves. Although loans from the IMF would have eased the pressure, American backing for this was essential and so Britain had to bow to Washington's demand for a ceasefire.
>
> The British had miscalculated, holding faulty perceptions of US policy: believed they would support or at least be indifferent, hoping at least for benign neutrality. Eisenhower summed up when he addressed the National Security Council on 1 November "How could we possibly support Britain and France and in doing so we lose the whole Arab world?"

Mr. X: Interestingly, Colonel Wilkerson, former Secretary of State Colin Powell's Chief of Staff, referenced exactly this UK Suez Moment in talking about the US in the passage earlier:

If that happens, a similar thing will happen to what Dwight Eisenhower threatened the British with, in the IMF, when they invaded Suez with the French and Israelis. The real powerful move that Ike made was to threaten a run on the [British] pound. Eden had to back off, he had to back off. He couldn't take that.

Luke: So, you're saying you think there are similarities between the then-global hegemon UK miscalculating what its allies would do in the Suez Crisis and current global hegemon US miscalculating what its allies might do in the Iran sanctions issue?

Mr. X: If I take what all these other nations are publicly saying at face value, then yes, I think there are similarities. What really gets my attention in this context is that virtually no one on Wall Street is thinking about this. There is an overwhelming consensus that the EU (and others) will simply acquiesce and permanently surrender their economic sovereignty to the US. But what if they don't? It sets up a very binary set of risks.

Luke: Could the UK's "Suez Moment" be instructive for the US' case, given the now multitude of warnings about the USD's primary reserve status if things are mishandled?

Mr. X: Yes, I think it could be instructive.

Luke: So, what are you watching to gauge what's happening?

Mr. X: Charles Gave of GaveKal gave a fascinating interview a few weeks ago on Macrovoices (https://www.macrovoices.com/400-charles-gave-our-industry-is-not-prepared-for-secular-inflation) recently on this topic; I happen to agree with his point.

Luke: Which was?

Mr. X: China wants to internationalize CNY through gold; the US does not want this to happen. He uses the phrase "The Upcoming Monetary War, with Gold as an Arbiter." More specifically, Charles Gave said this on that Macrovoices interview:

> CHARLES GAVE: Okay, you are China. You want to de-dollarize the world. So, you have to offer a credible alternative to the dollar. You want to de-dollarize not only trade between nations in Asia—if Korea was selling goods to Taiwan, they were settling their accounts, up to two or three years ago, in dollars. And the Chinese are saying, why on earth do we have to use the dollar to settle the account between us? So, they are trying to do that.
>
> They are also trying to de-dollarize the oil markets. That has started with Russia. Iran is now selling its oil in Euro. So, you have a lot of movement saying that there is something happening also in the oil markets.
>
> So, the Chinese want to de-dollarize. But now the problem is that they want also to keep their capital account closed. In simple words, that means that they want to control the money that comes in and out of China. So, it's difficult to tell people you should keep your reserves in renminbi if at the same time you prevent the guys from either investing in China or taking their money abroad. You see what I mean there.
>
> There is a very astute solution that the Chinese have found: It has been to say, guys, look, if you have too many renminbi because you have been selling a lot of oil to China, or whatever, we will settle either in renminbi, you can keep your renminbi in your reserves, fine with us. Or we can give you gold instead of renminbi.
>
> So, you have to understand that the gold price is now a big play between the US and China. For the Chinese currency

to be credible, a big rise in the price of gold would help them tremendously. Because they have been buying gold like crazy for the last six or seven years. So, they have huge inventories of gold. And that is what will ultimately lend a lot of credibility to their currency.

On the other hand, the Americans don't want that de-dollarization because that's part of their power. And so, what they are trying to do is prevent gold from going up. So, to a certain extent, the price of gold is going to tell you who is going to win in that effort to de-dollarize Asia. If gold goes up, it's China. If gold goes down, it's the US.

Mr. X: I agree with Charles—far from being "useless," going forward, I increasingly believe gold will be an important tell on the status of the global monetary system.

Luke: What's it telling us now?

Mr. X: Look at the five-year chart below of gold (top line at right) v. inverted US real rates (bottom line at right) and you tell me how the market's betting….

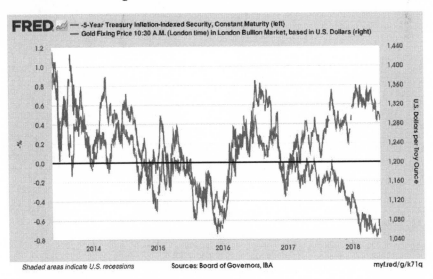

Luke: Fascinating…based on that chart, the market appears to have begun thinking sometime last year that China is getting the upper hand, even as *heavy* consensus in the US is that King USD will win.

Mr. X: Yes…if I was a speculator, I would want to own or be long currency volatility, gold volatility, and probably gold as a core position until this whole matter is settled.

Luke: Agreed. Well, we've covered a lot of ground once again. Why don't we stop there for now? Thanks again for reaching out to meet.

Mr. X: It was my pleasure, as always.

Chapter 5

TRUMP AND "THE MOST POWERFUL BUREAUCRAT IN EU HISTORY" JUST PUT USD-CENTRIC ENERGY/FOREIGN POLICY TENSIONS ON FULL DISPLAY

JULY 12, 2018

My next meeting with Mr. X took place in July 2018, in New York. I had landed at LaGuardia Airport that morning from Cleveland, and now found myself walking down Fifth Avenue toward Central Park to meet Mr. X at the venerable Knickerbocker Club. I had never been there before, but Mr. X had apparently long been a member, and he had reserved a private room so we could talk plainly.

Luke: Thank you for inviting me, Mr. X. It is great to see you again.

Mr. X: You're welcome. Thank you for coming to New York.

Luke: When we talked five weeks ago, I didn't anticipate talking to you again so soon. To what do I owe the pleasure of your visit?

Mr. X: I didn't anticipate meeting up so soon as well, but events appear to be accelerating. Yesterday, for the second time in a month, my jaw dropped while watching a CNBC excerpt of Trump meeting with NATO officials. Listen to what Trump said: [Mr. X pulled out a sheet of paper from his binder and read the following.]

> "So, we're protecting Germany and France from Russia, and they are paying billions of dollars to Russia for a gas pipeline...and I think that's very inappropriate; it doesn't make sense that they pay billions of dollars for gas to Russia, and we have to defend them against...Russia. I think trade is wonderful, but I think energy is a whole different story. I think energy is a much different story than normal trade."

> **President Trump has launched a scathing tirade ahead of the NATO summit – 7/11/18**

> https://twitter.com/CNBCi/status/101696929574883
> 7376

Luke: "Energy is a much different story than normal trade"? What could Trump possibly be referring to?

Mr. X: Well, that comment took me right back to a curious tweet made a month ago on June 10 by a man who has been called "the most powerful bureaucrat in EU history," with some even going so far as to say he is "the true leader of the European Union." I'm referring to Martin Selmayr, who said:

> On 8/15/71, Pres. Nixon used TV (a new medium at that time) to unilaterally end US commitment to the Bretton Woods system. Europe had to react, started work on a Monetary Union which eventually led to the €. Europe needs to take its destiny in its own hands.

Source:
https://twitter.com/martinselmayr/status/100576489
6766783488

Selmayr's tweet did not receive nearly the press that Trump's tirade at German NATO officials did, but in my eyes, it was every bit as significant. The "most powerful bureaucrat in EU history" openly stated that the raison d'etre for the EUR was the US' unilateral default on the Bretton Woods system (which was followed by the petrodollar), to give Europe the flexibility to "take its destiny in its own hands."

Curiously, as I have highlighted before, the EUR is not the only currency bloc that sees the US' unilateral default on the Bretton Woods system as a key moment in history. Chinese general Qiao Liang said something similar in a speech to Chinese Communist Party officials two years ago:

> According to the wishes of the Americans, the Bretton Woods system establishes the hegemonic position of the U.S. dollar. But in fact, after more than 20 years of practice, from 1944 to 1971, a full 27 years, it did not really allow Americans to gain hegemony. What blocked the hegemony of the dollar? It is gold.
>
> At that time, few people in the entire world could clearly see this point, including many economists and financial experts. They cannot very clearly point out that the most important incident in the 20th century was not World War I or World War II nor the Soviet Union. The most important event of the 20th century was the decoupling of the dollar from gold on August 15, 1971.

Luke: What do you make of these recent comments, in the context of the historical comments you've highlighted?

Mr. X: From the preceding, we can infer the following:

1. The US considers "energy" very different from "normal" trade.

2. The EUR was created in response to the US' unilateral default on the Bretton Woods system.

3. At least some portion of Chinese officials also see the US' unilateral default on the Bretton Woods system as a critically-important event.

Furthermore, we know the US was trying to convince the EU as far back as 2002 not to hook up with the Russians on energy. On July 11, 2018, former White House Press Secretary Ari Fleischer stated:

> In 2002 in Berlin, Pres. Bush told Chancellor Schroeder directly that Schroeder's decision to phase out nuclear power meant he was turning Germany's energy security over to Russia. Little did anyone know Schroeder would go on to become chairman of Rosneft.

And on May 16, 2014, former Secretary of State Condoleezza Rice said:

> We need to have tougher sanctions [on Russia], & at some point this is probably going to have to involve oil and gas.... Over the long run, you simply want to change the structure of energy dependence, you want to depend more on the N. American energy platform, the tremendous bounty of oil & gas we are finding in North America. You want to have pipelines that don't go through Ukraine & Russia. For years, we've been trying to get the Europeans interested in different pipeline routes. It's time to do that.

And we also know that from at least as far back as 2010, Russia has found attractive the potential to both a) become economically closer to the EU, and b) move away from the USD's monopoly on the pricing of its biggest exports (energy, as was so eloquently described by Senator John McCain in 2014 when he said this):

> Russia is a gas station masquerading as a country.

Vladimir Putin verified this when he stated in November 2010:

> Can it be supposed that one day Russia will be in some joint currency zone with Europe? Yes, quite possible.... We should move away from the excessive monopoly of the dollar as the only global reserve currency.

Reuters, on August 14, 2014, also documented Putin as saying:

> Russia should aim to sell its oil and gas for rubles globally because the dollar monopoly in energy trade was damaging Russia's economy. "We should act carefully. At the moment we are trying to agree with some countries to trade in national currencies."

Luke: This is all interesting, so I must ask: What do you see as the common thread tying all of these quotes from different officials together?

Mr. X: Allow me to put it together. In my view, from these quotes, we can infer that:

1. The EU doesn't like the petrodollar system (or else it never would've formed the EUR.)

2. China doesn't like the petrodollar system.

3. Russia doesn't like the petrodollar system.

4. The US sees energy trade associated with the petrodollar system as "different from normal trade."

Luke: Okay, I can see that common thread now that you lay it out. But that then leaves me wondering what is underlying numbers 1-4 above in each case? Why do these nations or regions feel this way?

Mr. X: The national security of all involved: The EU, China, and Russia don't like their energy import (China, EU) and export (Russia) tabs effectively being at the whims of the US government and Fed (especially understanding that US structural deficits must expand to fund US entitlements in coming years), while the US knows it needs USD energy surpluses to be recycled into US financial markets to afford ever-growing Entitlement and DoD-driven deficits.

Furthermore, both the EU and Russia have an additional clear and present complicating factor to add to the analysis above:

> Netherlands to begin reducing production at Europe's biggest gas field Groningen, fully halt Groningen production by 2030.
>
> **– Reuters, 3/29/18**

> Russia's challenge is...its demographic decline is so steep, so far advanced, and so multi-vectored that for demographic reasons alone Russia is unlikely to survive as a state, and Russians are unlikely to survive as a people over the next couple of generations. Yet within Russia's completely indefensible borders, it cannot possibly last even that long. Russia has at most eight years of relative strength to act. **– Analyst Peter Zeihan, 2014**

Luke: Wait, Europe's biggest gas field is going into decline *now* and production will be halted entirely in twelve years...?

Mr. X: Yes...and that's arguably the smaller and more distant problem of the two! As Peter Zeihan noted in 2014, "Russia is unlikely to survive as a state" and "has at most eight years of

112

relative strength to act"! In other words, the Europeans are increasingly going to run out of domestic gas starting today while by Zeihan's count, the Russians have at most four years to act to avoid possibly ceasing to exist as a state.

Luke: "Other than that, how was the play Mrs. Lincoln?", I guess.

Mr. X: Zeihan thinks Russia needs to act, but he also thinks Russia must act kinetically via military action to avoid this fate; I think Zeihan is missing something much more subtle and elegant, but no less effective. For that, I go to two sets of quotes I've shared with you multiple times; first from the former chief of staff for Secretary of State Colin Powell, Colonel Lawrence Wilkerson; and then from a Russian analyst, both of which tie in both the EU and Russia's clear and present problems:

> "What they want to do is use Putin and others' oil power, Petrodollars if you will, and I say that PetroYuan, PetroRenminbi, PetroEuro, whatever, to force the US to lose its incredibly powerful role of owning the world's transactional action reserve currency.

> **– Col. Lawrence Wilkerson, fmr. Chief of Staff to Sec. State Colin Powell – 10/8/14**

Not long ago, British scientists [and] the U.S. Geological Survey concluded Europe will not be able to survive without energy supply from Russia, [which means] "The world will not be able to survive if oil and gas from Russia is subtracted from the global balance of energy supply".

Thus, the Western world, built on the hegemony of the petrodollar, is in a catastrophic situation in which it cannot survive without oil and gas supplies from Russia! And Russia is now ready to sell its oil and gas to the West only in exchange for physical gold!

The twist of Putin's game is that the mechanism for the sale of Russian energy to the West only for gold now works regardless of whether the West agrees to pay for Russian oil and gas with its artificially cheap gold, or not....

In 1971, US President Richard Nixon closed the 'gold window', ending the free exchange of dollars for gold, guaranteed by the US in 1944 at Bretton Woods. In 2014, Russian President Vladimir Putin has reopened the 'gold window', without asking Washington's permission.

– **Analyst Dmitry Kalinichenko, 11/23/14**

Luke: When we first started talking about this dynamic at FFTT, we sometimes had people laugh at us. However, as time has passed, we have simply showed them this chart. [I passed Mr. X the chart below.] When we do, they stop laughing.

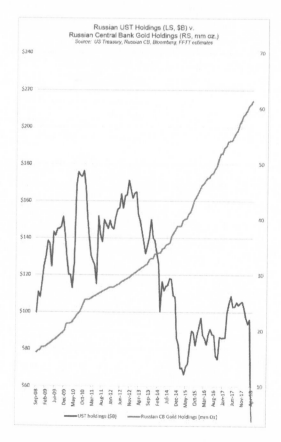

Mr. X: I don't know who Kalinichenko is, but what he described in 2014 has been happening in spades [describing the chart before].

Whether we look at that Russian gold v. UST chart you just handed me, or what China's been doing vis-à-vis gold imports [handing me the chart below]:

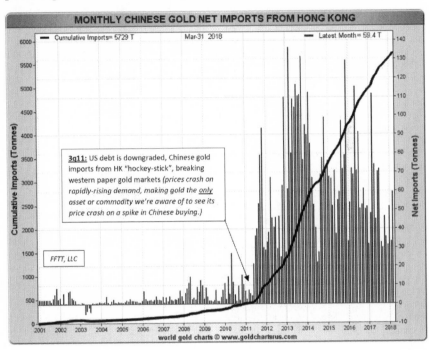

Mr. X: Or that global Central Banks have bought nearly eight times more gold than USTs since 2013, led by Russia and China... ✓

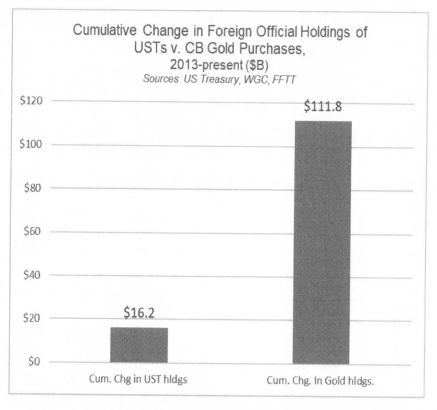

Cumulative Change in Foreign Official Holdings of
USTs v. CB Gold Purchases,
2013-present ($B)
Sources: US Treasury, WGC, FFTT

...and note that this chart does not include any of these EU gold repatriations [He read off the following list of headlines]:

> Netherlands repatriates gold, becoming the latest EU country to address concerns about safety of its gold
>
> – *WSJ*, **11/21/14**
>
> Austria to repatriate some gold from London
>
> – **Reuters, 5/28/15**
>
> Germany repatriates gold stashed abroad during cold war
>
> – **FT, 8/23/17**

Mr. X: Do you see it?

Luke: At the risk of seeming thick, no I do not.

Mr. X: Oh, Luke, you are not thick. I'll spell it out: Russia, China, and the EU have been quietly but steadily using energy to weaponize gold against the USD. In this way, all three can resolve the aforementioned energy/USD balance of payments problems, but only if gold is allowed to rise as "energy bids for physical gold." To date, though, gold has *not* risen. Why not?

As a major physical gold trader told me earlier this year, the answer is "It's been being papered over." While there is not great data on physical gold market leverage, the little data that does exist suggests physical gold paper leverage has been steadily rising since 2013. [Mr. X handed me the chart below to illustrate his point.]

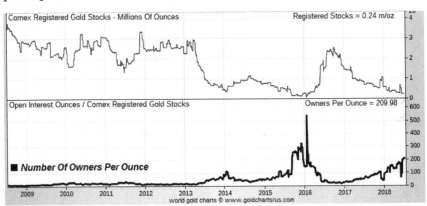

Mr. X: What this suggests is that a new "London Gold Pool" of sorts is developing, where "someone" has been pegging the price of gold in the $1150-1350/oz. range for more than five years by increasing paper leverage on a falling amount of physical gold.

Luke: So like we've been saying, none of what these other nations are doing will matter to the gold price until it matters?

Mr. X: Precisely. None of the preceding regarding Russian, Chinese, and EU weaponization of gold against the USD will matter...until it matters. And Martin Selmayr reminded us of how it came to "matter" at the end of the last London Gold Pool:

> On 8/15/71, Nixon used TV (a new medium) to unilaterally end US commitment to the Bretton Woods system. Europe had to react, started work on a Monetary Union which eventually led to the €. Europe needs to take its destiny in its own hands.

> **– Martin Selmayr, "Most powerful bureaucrat in EU history," Secretary General of EU, 6/10/18**

However, as we move toward it "mattering," in theory, one would expect to see symptoms; the chart below (gold v. US real rates, 2013-present) of gold ceasing to fall on rising US real rates would be a possible symptom, as foreign investors began putting money into gold regardless of what real rates are doing, perhaps expecting real rates to decline in coming months. But let's see how this develops....

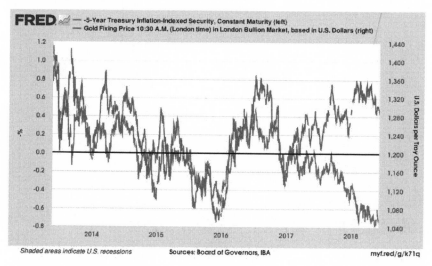

Luke: Agreed. Well, we've covered a lot of ground once again. Why don't we stop there for now? Thanks again for reaching out to meet.

Mr. X: It was my pleasure, as always.

Chapter 6

A US/CHINA TRADE WAR? THE FIRST ROUND'S ALREADY OVER, AND THE US LOST... BUT THE SECOND ROUND IS NOW STARTING

JULY 19, 2018

Just one week after Mr. X and I met in New York, my phone rang; it was Mr. X.

"Luke, are you in Cleveland?"

"Yes."

"Would you like some company this afternoon?"

"I'd love some!"

Mr. X had apparently had some business to take care of in Detroit that morning, so he decided to swing down to see me on the west side of Cleveland. He arrived at my office a little after lunch time.

Luke: Thank you for joining me again, Mr. X. It is great to see you.

Mr. X: You're welcome. Thank you for hosting me.

Luke: When I talked to you last week, I didn't anticipate talking to you again so soon. To what do I owe the pleasure of your visit?

Mr. X: Well, all of a sudden, it seems I'm hearing about the US/China trade war as if it's some new phenomenon, so I wanted to share some thoughts with you, if I might.

Luke: Of course. I'm always happy to talk about the world with you. What's on your mind?

Mr. X: In my view, pundits debating who is going to win a trade war between the US and China are missing the forest for the trees. Facts on the ground suggest that the first round of the US/China trade war is over, and on a net basis, the US lost—but there were clear winners and losers within the US. Given the highest wealth inequality in the US since 1929, it would seem "the 1%" won, while the US working and middle classes lost.

A stark visualization of the outcome of the casualties of what I would call "Round 1 of the China/US trade war" can be seen in the deaths of "economic hopelessness" that have gripped wide swaths of the US over the past twenty years.

For example, for the first time in fifty-five years, US life expectancy has declined two years in a row, driven by a staggering increase in "deaths of economic hopelessness"—suicide, alcohol, drug overdoses, and chronic liver disease. [Mr. X shared with me some articles and charts to back up his point.]

> **Life expectancy in America has declined for 2 years in a row, the 1st time that has happened since 1962-63 – 1/4/18**
>
> https://www.economist.com/united-states/2018/01/04/life-expectancy-in-america-has-declined-for-two-years-in-a-row

Death rates rising for middle aged white Americans – 11/3/15

http://mobile.nytimes.com/2015/11/03/health/death-rates-rising-for-middle-aged-white-americans-study-finds.html

Luke: Wow...grim and startling statistics. What changed beginning around 1999 that drove such elevated levels of "economic hopelessness"?

Mr. X: Well, at the tail end of the 2001 recession, China was granted "Most Favored Nation" status in the World Trade Organization or WTO...after which the US manufacturing sector promptly shed roughly 6 million jobs over the next seven years. [He handed me the next chart and continued to hand me charts and articles as he spoke.]

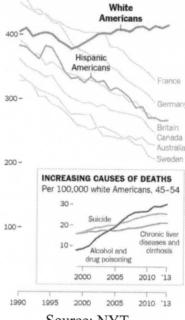

Dying in Middle Age

Death rates are rising for middle-aged white Americans, while declining in other wealthy countries and among other races and ethnicities. The rise appears to be driven by suicide, drugs and alcohol abuse.

Source: NYT

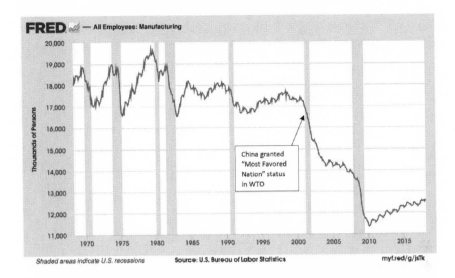

And so, given the sudden need to compete with cheap Chinese labor, labor's share of US economic output unsurprisingly collapsed right along with US manufacturing jobs:

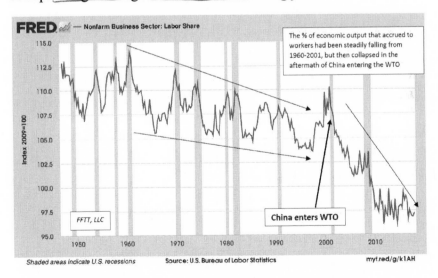

Luke: Presumably, there were some winners in the US economy as the US middle and working classes lost?

Mr. X: Of course. For example, US corporate profits as a percentage of GDP rose to their highest levels in the post-war era (at least until 2006, which is the cut-off date of this chart)....

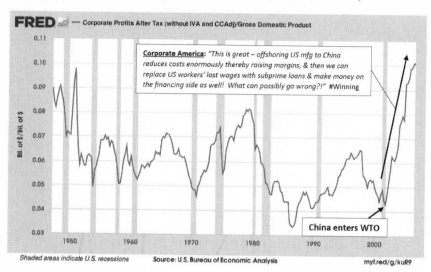

While government payrolls rose to help offset the loss of manufacturing jobs....

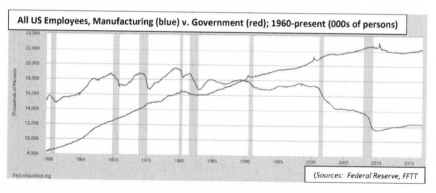

And rapidly-rising Chinese UST holdings taken on as part of the WTO deal [chart at right] meant exporters of USTs (i.e., the Washington, DC, region) saw their relative wealth grow rapidly versus that of the rest of the US:

7 of nations' 10 most affluent counties are now in the Washington DC region – 9/19/12

https://www.washingtonpost.com/local/seven-of-nations-10-most-affluent-counties-are-in-washington-region/2012/09/19/f580bf30-028b-11e2-8102-ebee9c66e190_story.html?utm_term=.2271d3115197

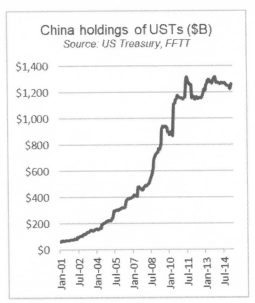

Luke: So what happened to upset the prior arrangement whereby US labor lost while corporate America and Washington won? The annotated chart you showed me before of corporate profit margins as a percentage of GDP continuing forward ended with 2006. What does that look like from 2006 to the present day?

Mr. X: A perfect segue, Luke…. Here it is, with its own additional annotations for the 2006 to present time frame!

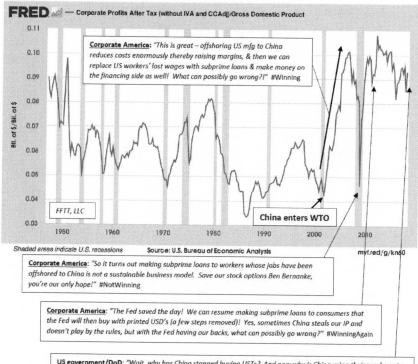

Shaded areas indicate U.S. recessions   Source: U.S. Bureau of Economic Analysis   myf.red/g/kn50

Luke: So what do you think has changed to drive the seeming "awakening" going on in Washington, DC?

Mr. X: This excellent chart by Taylor Mann [He handed me the chart on the next page] likely highlights a critical forcing function on the sudden shift in the US' strategy/tactics we inferred in the prior annotated chart: You cannot squeeze blood from a stone, and after years of operating an economic system that effectively did exactly that to much of US "flyover country" (ultimately leading to the worst economic crisis in eighty years), the worm turned— Western voters have begun expressing their displeasure at the ballot boxes:

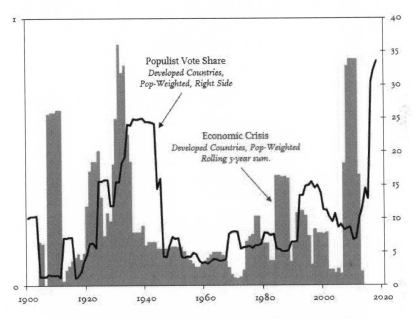

FIG. V. THE BACKLASH: POPULIST VOTE SHARE *vs.* ECONOMIC CRISIS

Australia, Austria, Belgium, Canada, Denmark, Finland, France, Germany, Greece, Ireland, Italy, Japan, Netherlands, Norway, Spain, Sweden, Switzerland, United Kingdom, United States.

Source: Taylor Mann,
https://twitter.com/Mann_Major/status/998712158308519938

Mr. X: The problem for the US system as currently structured is that corporate America and US top executives have been among the biggest beneficiaries of growth in the Chinese economy—first, as a source of low cost labor to bolster margins, and now, more recently, as a sizable portion of US multinational corporate sales. [Mr. X pulled out an article and read from it.]

US corporations/multinationals have $1.4T "sales surplus" with world, $20B with China – 6/12/18

https://www.bloomberg.com/news/articles/2018-06-12/the-1-4-trillion-u-s-surplus-that-trump-s-not-talking-about

> "US companies have sold more to the rest of the world than other countries have sold to the US in the past ten years," writes chief China economist Zhang Zhiwei in the report.

> For China, the image of a massive trade deficit with the US "is at odds with the fact that Chinese consumers own more iPhones and buy more General Motors cars than US consumers," wrote Zhang in the report. "These cars and phones are sold to China not through US exports but through Chinese subsidiaries of multinational enterprises."

> Instead of a growing trade deficit with China, Deutsche Bank estimates there was a small but growing surplus.

This article raises a critical question.

Luke: Which is what?

Mr. X: Given the above, if US corporations are running a $1.4 trillion "sales surplus" with the rest of the world and a $20B (and rapidly-growing) "sales surplus" with China, how can the US cushion the blow to corporate America of a trade war, especially if (as we hypothesize) the US government/DoD now sees China as a threat to the US? This calculus is further complicated by the fact that corporate profits, due to US tax reforms, were basically flat year-over-year in the first quarter of 2018. [He showed me the following chart and article.]

Corporate profits weaker than they seem, down 6% y/y in 1q18 ex-tax reform benefits – 5/30/18

https://www.wsj.com/articles/why-corporate-profits-may-be-weaker-than-they-seem-1527701696

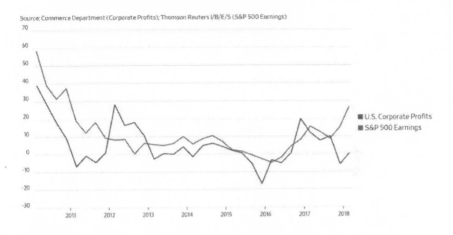

Source: Commerce Department (Corporate Profits); Thomson Reuters I/B/E/S (S&P 500 Earnings)

Source: WSJ

Luke: I don't know. How can the US cushion the blow to corporate America of a trade war with China?

Mr. X: I don't know either, but I would think a big corporate tax cut might be a good start; wouldn't you? [He handed me the below article to back up his point.]

Trump calls for another round of tax cuts, further reductions to corporate tax rate – 6/29/18

https://www.washingtonpost.com/news/business/wp/2018/06/29/trump-calls-for-another-round-of-tax-cuts-further-reductions-to-corporate-tax-rate/?utm_term=.434c1f47c48d

> President Trump on Friday said he wanted to further lower the corporate tax rate, from 21 percent to 20 percent, as part of a second round of tax cuts later this year.

Trump said the tax plan would be ready by October, "maybe a little sooner than that."

Luke: Yes, that would be a good start. Well, we've covered a lot of ground once again. Why don't we stop there for now? Thanks again for reaching out to meet.

Mr. X: It was my pleasure, as always.

Chapter 7

FIRST CURRENT ACCOUNT DEFICIT IN TWENTY-PLUS YEARS MEANS CHINA NO LONGER HAS THE LUXURY OF "PLAYING THE LONG GAME"

AUGUST 2, 2018

"Events must be accelerating," I thought as I looked at my phone ringing on my desk, flashing Mr. X's name. "Hello, Mr. X!" I answered.

"Luke, can you drive up to Detroit this afternoon? I'm back here today for a meeting and would love to catch up with you again, if you can make it."

"What's the address?" After scribbling the name of a restaurant down on the calendar on my desk, I said, "I'll be there in three hours."

Just under three hours later, I walked into the restaurant at the address Mr. X had given me. Since it was mid-afternoon on a weekday, the restaurant was mostly empty, so I quickly saw Mr. X in a booth. He waved to me, and I walked briskly over.

Mr. X: Luke, thanks for coming up on such short notice.

Luke: Getting to Detroit is easy, especially with the way people drive in Detroit—gotta love people going 85 miles an hour in the left lane!

Mr. X: Yes, I would imagine that does make the trip much quicker!

Luke: So what's going on?

Mr. X: Something I noticed in my readings recently. The overwhelming consensus appears to be that China is content to play "the long game" as it relates to US/Chinese trade tensions. There's just one problem with this narrative: China's first current account deficit in twenty-plus years means *China does not have the luxury of playing "the long game."*

This chart [at right] might be the most important chart in global finance right now because it suggests China must act quickly and possibly dramatically—a reality that does not appear to be well-understood by most market participants.

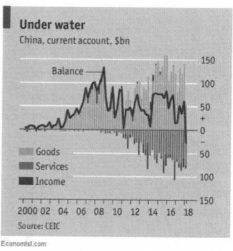

This chart should be at the forefront of every discussion of every financial media and macro analyst in the world…*yet it's not.* Instead, as noted by BAML, the number one "tail risk" being focused on by investors is "US/China trade tensions."

That global fund managers are focused on a Chinese trade war and not China's current account deficit is a divergence that has our "Spidey sense" tingling in a manner it rarely has in the past twenty-plus years for two reasons. Investors don't seem to realize that:

1. The so-called US/China "trade war" is merely a symptom of a much bigger issue.

2. China's current account deficit means this "much bigger issue" may come to a head sooner than most think.

Luke: Let's go back to the chart you showed me previously. [I pulled out the chart on the right]. China ran its first current account deficit in twenty-plus years in the first quarter of 2018. Why did this happen?

Mr. X: It was driven in no small part by a rapidly-growing services deficit, which is rising largely due to rapidly-growing Chinese tourism. [Mr. X pulled out an article and quoted from it.]

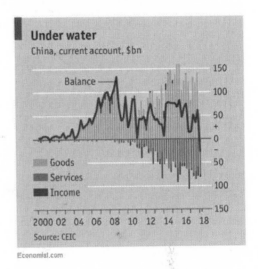

Under water
China, current account, $bn

China's tourism boom cause of shrinking current acct surplus – 6/13/18

https://jingtravel.com/chinas-tourism-boom-cause-of-shrinking-account-surplus/

Chinese tourists made 130 million trips abroad and spent $115.29 billion last year and the growth of these figures shows no signs of stopping. While it is undeniably yet another expression of China's growing global economic influence, tourism outflows will be something that Beijing will likely have to address in regards to the country's current account for years to come.

Mr. X: Let's now turn our attention to Chinese trade balances. [He pulled out the following two charts to show me.] When we look at the trade side of the equation, we find that according to MIT's Atlas database, China was a net exporter (i.e., trade surplus) of $1.04T in 2016 (latest data). Note that China's trade surplus has risen since 2014 as imports have fallen, likely aided significantly by falling commodity prices....

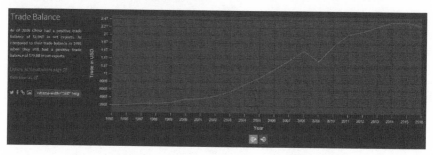

Source: http://atlas.media.mit.edu/en/profile/country/chn/

After all, more than 60 percent of China's $1.23T of imports in 2016 were raw commodities (8 percent alone was oil):

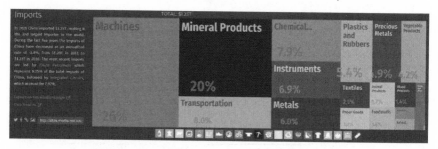

Source: http://atlas.media.mit.edu/en/profile/country/chn/

So, when we take a step back to see the forest for the trees, as you like to say, here's what we see:

1. China's growing services deficit driven heavily by tourism.

2. China's growing trade surplus aided significantly by falling commodity prices since 2014.

Luke: Okay, go on…

Mr. X: That brings us to two final pieces of the puzzle for China in the context of the first Chinese current account deficit in twenty-plus years:

1. China's energy consumption (and likely total commodity consumption) is growing strongly (energy up 6.8 percent year-over-year according to Bloomberg data) [below], and…

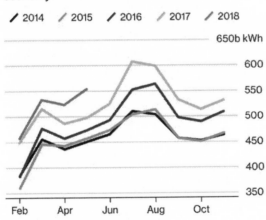

Heading for the Peak

China's energy consumption grows along with the economy

/ 2014   / 2015   / 2016   / 2017   / 2018

Source: National Energy Administration

2. Crude oil prices in particular are up nearly 70 percent since 6/29/17, when President Trump announced the US' "Energy Dominance Strategy." [chart below]

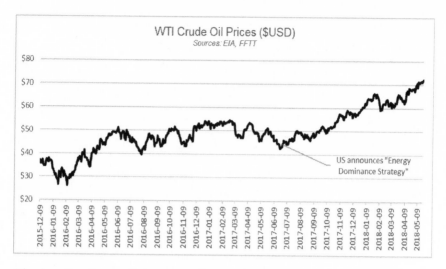

The implications of the preceding series of charts are critical to understand.

Luke: Why?

Mr. X: China running a sustained current account deficit could be problematic to the Chinese yuan and, therefore, to Chinese authorities. However, this implies that unless China either…

1. Limits Chinese outbound tourism (which would likely run counter to domestic Chinese political goals), or

2. Slashes commodity imports further (likely limiting economic growth and again running counter to domestic Chinese political goals),

…then China's current account deficit is likely to continue to worsen from here.

This decision tree flow chart highlights why a structural Chinese current account deficit could be problematic, and the steps China could take to combat it. [He passed me the chart below.]

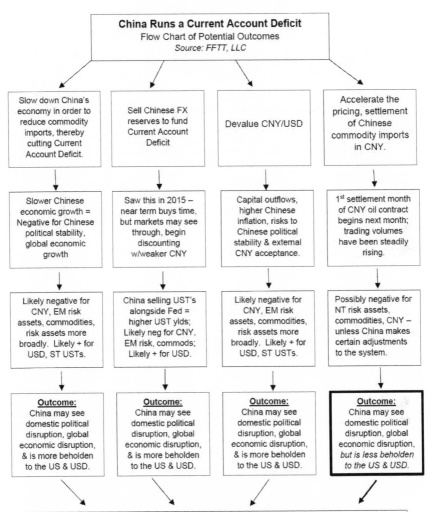

"Avoiding disruption" may no longer be on the menu of options for China: Western pundits' base case appears to be that China will *"play the long game"* to *"avoid domestic political instability & global economic instability."*

However, what this flow chart shows is once China runs a current account deficit, *"avoiding domestic political & global economic instability"* is likely unavoidable. As such, China's choice is not *"to avoid instability or not,"* but rather *"to remain beholden to the US & USD-centric system or not."* (bolded bottom box at right).

Our bet is China will choose *"not beholden,"* an option few Western pundits realize China even has, much less are prepared or positioned for. Critically, China's current account deficit may serve as a forcing function to this decision, sooner rather than later.

Luke: Wow. So you think "avoiding disruption" may no longer be on the menu of options for China? That they no longer have the luxury of playing "the long game"?

Mr. X: No. I am betting China will choose disruption, but no longer be beholden to the US and USD to deal with their seemingly-looming current account-deficit problem.

Luke: Why?

Mr. X: Because I'm watching what they're saying and doing…. [He read me excerpts from the next couple of articles.]

> **China taking first steps to pay for oil in CNY this year: sources – 3/29/18**
>
> https://www.reuters.com/article/us-china-oil-yuan-exclusive/exclusive-china-taking-first-steps-to-pay-for-oil-in-yuan-this-year-sources-idUSKBN1H51FA
>
>> Shifting just part of global oil trade into the yuan is potentially huge. Oil is the world's most traded commodity, with an annual trade value of around $14 trillion, roughly equivalent to China's gross domestic product last year.
>>
>> A pilot program for yuan payment could be launched as early as the second half of this year, two of the people said.
>>
>> Regulators have informally asked a handful of financial institutions to prepare for pricing China's crude imports in the yuan, said the three sources at some of the financial firms.
>>
>> "Being the biggest buyer of oil, it's only natural for China to push for the usage of yuan for payment

THE MR. X INTERVIEWS

settlement. This will also improve the yuan liquidity in the global market," said one of the people briefed on the matter by Chinese authorities.

Under the plan being discussed, Beijing could possibly start with purchases from Russia and Angola, one of the people said, although the source had no details of anything in the works.

If successful, it could also trigger shifting other product payments to CNY, including metals and mining raw materials.

Top African finance officials discuss possible use of CNY as reserve currency for eastern, southern Africa – 5/29/18

http://www.xinhuanet.com/english/2018-05/29/c_137213337.htm

According to Ole S. Hansen of Saxo Bank:

"Most countries in the MEFMI region have loans or grants from China and it would only make economic sense to repay in renminbi (Chinese yuan). This is the reason why it is critical for policy makers to strategize on progress that the continent has made to embrace the Chinese yuan which has become what may be termed 'common currency' in trade with Africa.

"Ascendancy of Chinese yuan in the Special Drawing Rights (SDR) basket of currencies is an important symbol of its importance and IMF's approval as an official reserve currency.

"17 weeks after being launched, China's petro-yuan continues to take market share from Brent & WTI. Despite its much shorter trading hours (9.5 vs 23) the four-week average market share rose above 11% last week."

Mr. X: In light of the chart below, it is noteworthy that the first settlement month of China's CNY oil contract is next month—September—just as China's current account deficit issue is coming to a head.

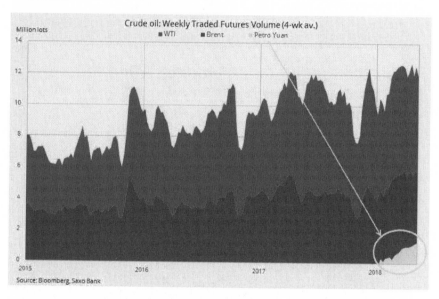

Then, as I was getting ready to come see you, this potentially *enormous* signal hit newswires (h/t DC):

(Bloomberg, 8/2/18) — China will orderly realize yuan capital account convertibility and protect interests of foreign investors, State Administration of Foreign Exchange [SAFE] says in a statement.

- SAFE will improve supervision system for cross-border capital flow

- SAFE will crack down on transaction fraud, underground banking and safeguard national economic and financial security
- SAFE will preserve and increase value of forex [foreign exchange] reserves

Luke: What grabbed you most about this story?

Mr. X: That last line: "SAFE will preserve and increase value of forex reserves."

Luke: How could they do that?

Mr. X: *The Wall Street Journal* has been noticing this correlation between gold and Chinese yuan since June 2017.

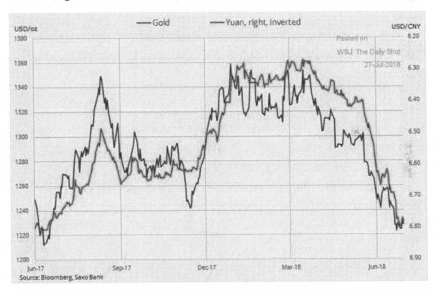

Gold priced in Chinese yuan has been quite stable over the past 6-9 months, which left us wondering:

Did SAFE (China) just tell us that "we are going to keep the price of gold in yuan stable-to-rising" when it said "SAFE will preserve and increase value of forex reserves"?

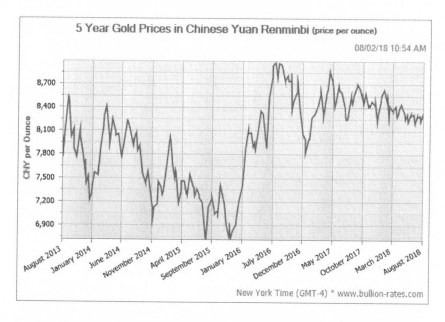

Luke: So, what do you think the signaling value of that SAFE statement could be?

Mr. X: What would happen to the yuan value of global FX reserves if SAFE "preserving and increasing the value of forex reserves" meant increasing the yuan price of gold?

Well, Russia, for one, would see its purchasing power in yuan terms rise (gold holdings up and to the right).

Furthermore, given that the first physical settlement month of the yuan oil contract is next month, Russia's outright dumping of USTs in the last two months is somewhat auspicious:

Russian UST Holdings (LS, $B) v.
Russian Central Bank Gold Holdings (RS, mm oz.)
Source: US Treasury, Russian CB, Bloomberg, FFTT estimates

Mr. X: And you have repeatedly noted that Russia has led global central banks in their post-2010 change in gold purchases, which has accelerated to the point where in the past five years, global central banks have bought significantly more gold than USTs in aggregate. [He handed me the chart at right.]

Cumulative Change in Foreign Official Holdings of USTs v. CB Gold Purchases, 2013-present ($B)
Sources: US Treasury, WGC, FFTT

Critically, this chart does not include any central bank repatriations of gold (such as those conducted by several nations in the EU, including Germany, Austria, and the Netherlands.)

Luke: So what is the bottom line in your view?

Mr. X: The bottom line is that if gold rises in CNY terms, the CNY reserves (& CNY purchasing power) of any global Central Bank with gold will also rise. Something big appears to be happening here, even as many Western investors expect China simply to roll over and acquiesce to the US and USD system. We are watching these developments closely.

Luke: It will be interesting to see what happens. Thank you again, Mr. X for the information. It was a pleasure to talk to you again.

Mr. X: It's my pleasure to talk with you again, Luke.

Chapter 8

NEGATIVE FX-HEDGED UST YIELDS FOR FOREIGN INVESTORS = RISK OFF, USD UP, RATES UP UNTIL USD IS DEVALUED

OCTOBER 18, 2018

I was at my desk on a beautiful early fall day in Cleveland when my phone rang unexpectedly. I glanced at the number and saw it was Mr. X.

Luke: What a pleasant surprise to hear from you again, Mr. X. What's going on?

Mr. X: Hi, Luke. I'm going to be in town tomorrow night for a meeting—any chance you could meet up for dinner? It's really important.

Luke: Of course—I'd love to. What's going on?

Mr. X: We can talk more about it tomorrow night, but in the meantime, check out this John Dizard article in the *Financial Times* last Friday, October 12. I thought it was really important. I'll email it to you right now.

Luke: Okay, I just got it; I'll take a look. Why do you think it was so important?

Mr. X: It strongly suggests that unless the USD weakens notably and soon, either UST yields may begin rising surprisingly sharply as foreign buyers may no longer find it attractive to roll-over some portion of the $7-8 trillion in USTs the US needs to roll in the next twelve months because FX-hedged UST yields are now negative, or US and global risk assets may begin selling off sharply as US government borrowing crowds out risk assets globally.

Luke: Whoa! What was the title of the article, and what did it say? [As I finished asking, the article hit my email inbox]:

> **Foreigners can no longer underwrite US economic expansion – 10/12/18**
>
> https://www.ft.com/content/8e345bdc-4bbf-32bb-ac73-3610a338efdd

Mr. X: The title was quite direct—"Foreigners can no longer underwrite US economic expansion"—and its subtitle was perhaps even more so: "America's' 'free lunch' is over as regulators urge reduction in swaps exposure."

Luke: Dang! That is pretty direct, especially for a British publication!

Mr. X: Agreed. And as direct as the title was, the body of the article only continued the body blows. Listen to this:

> You know those bells that are supposed to never ring to signal a turn in the market? Well, they started ringing on September 27 and 28. On that Thursday and Friday, just before the end of the third quarter, the interbank market's cross-currency "basis swap" for euros to US dollars rose by 30 basis points. In the same period, the cost of yen-dollar basis swaps went up by 46 basis points.

That was the end of foreigners paying for the US's economic expansion. It also probably marked the end of the housing recovery.

Luke: Wow…you're right—not pulling any punches.

Mr. X: No…and it gets better.

The effect of those changes in the basis swap rates was to make it uneconomic for European or Japanese investors to buy US Treasury bonds and hedge away the currency risk.

That such trades were possible would appear to violate the "no-arbitrage principle" of financial economics, but then America usually gets a free lunch from the rest of the world.

Luke: Man, you weren't kidding. Dizard is just whaling away on the US….

Mr. X: Hold on—listen to this part:

All this made it possible for non-US institutions to hold large bond positions that paid a positive rate of interest without incurring any foreign exchange risk. This may appear to be a sort of financial magic, but the foreign exchange risk did not go away. It just continued to grow as an irradiated part of the banks' derivatives book that had been hidden in plain sight.

Luke: "…a sort of financial magic" that "continued to grow as an irradiated part of the banks' derivatives book." How fast have FX swaps grown?

Mr. X: Tell you what. Hold that thought, and we'll pick this up at dinner tomorrow night, all right?

Luke: Sounds good. See you then.

The next night, I headed to Lola, the Michael Symon restaurant in Cleveland's East 4th Street district; Mr. X walked in shortly after I arrived. We sat down and began our discussion.

Mr. X: Last night, you asked me, "How fast have FX swaps grown?" The answer to your question appears to be "quite rapidly." [Handing me the chart below.] FX swaps with maturities of less than one year have grown from $22T to $50T (notional) in only eight years!

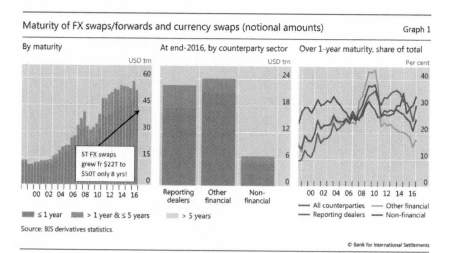

Maturity of FX swaps/forwards and currency swaps (notional amounts) — Graph 1

Source: BIS derivatives statistics.

© Bank for International Settlements

Mr. X: Dizard discusses this BIS report in the *Financial Times* article, noting that they identified a problem but hesitated to really "call out" the problem in plain language:

> By September last year, though, central bank researchers had estimated what they called "the missing foreign debt" that had been financing the relatively strong US recovery. According to a special report by the Bank for International Settlements, the "missing" debt was in excess of the $10.7tn in cash market valuations.
>
> The BIS estimated in 2016 that "the missing debt amounts to some $13-$14tn but the implications for financial

stability are quite subtle and require an assessment of both currency and maturity mismatches".

Luke: "The missing debt amounts to some $13-14 trillion but the implications for financial stability are quite subtle"? Classic central bank-speak...

Mr. X: For sure. Luckily, Dizard not only translated the BIS' "central bank-speak" into plain English...

> To sum up those "subtle implications": the US had borrowed an extra $14tn or so, and the currency risk assumed by the foreigners lending this money had been principally covered by the US banking system, which had underestimated how dangerous this could be.

...but also made sure to clarify why this story may be so important *now*:

> Anecdotally, as the end of the third quarter of this year approached, the regulators leaning over the large banks' trading desks indicated that it would be a good idea to cut back on all that swaps exposure.

Luke: So, with the preceding excerpts as context, can you summarize for our readers why this story got your attention to the point that you picked up the phone and called me?

Mr. X: Sure. I'll be blunt. What this story means is that unless something changes *very* rapidly with cross-currency basis swaps, USTs are likely to have a supply/demand mismatch while UST auctions are likely to get increasingly sloppy.

Luke: Why is that, and why now?

Mr. X: The "why" can be seen in an excerpt from the Bloomberg stories from the last two weeks.... I'll email it to you later, but let me read it to you now. [He read me the following, emphasizing the key parts.]

10y UST yields just turned negative for European buyers – 9/27/18

https://www.bloomberg.com/news/articles/2018-09-27/treasury-10-year-yields-just-turned-negative-for-european-buyers

Bond Traders Are Paid Big to Dump U.S. Treasuries and Go Abroad – 10/17/18

https://www.bloomberg.com/news/articles/2018-10-17/bond-traders-get-paid-big-to-dump-u-s-treasuries-and-go-abroad

> But more than just being a savvy trade idea, it underscores how *the longstanding and popular narrative of the U.S. as a go-to destination for yield-seeking bond investors is little more than an illusion.*
>
> While U.S. investors have few incentives to stay at home, the sky-high cost for foreigners to hedge the dollar means they have little cause to buy Treasuries. In some cases, their effective *yields* can fall below zero. Any letup in demand could drive up U.S. borrowing costs, at a time when the government can ill-afford to lose investors as it raises ever more debt to meet its widening budget deficits. (Of course, bond investors can always opt not to hedge, though making a bet on the direction of currencies entails an added risk.)

The answer to your question "why now" is hinted at in the Dizard *Financial Times* article:

> Anecdotally, as the end of the third quarter of this year approached, the regulators leaning over the large banks'

trading desks indicated that it would be a good idea to cut back on all that swaps exposure.

The tightening in USD liquidity manifested by cross-currency basis swaps can be seen in another chart. [He handed me the chart below.] You can see that despite the breakout in UST yields, on an FX-hedged basis, UST yields are nominally negative:

Luke: So, because FX-hedged UST yields are negative, foreign private buyers are not interested in buying new UST issuance?

Mr. X: Correct, but the problem is much, *much* bigger than that. In fact, I would argue that unless FX-hedged UST yields turn positive very soon, they may quickly represent a threat to US national security!

Luke: Why?

Mr. X: Luke, you should know the answer to that better than most!

Luke: I'm not sure I follow....

Mr. X: Luke, your report a couple of months ago noted that the US needs to "roll" $7-8 trillion in USTs in the next twelve months... [He handed me the following chart]

Sources of Privately-Held Financing in Fiscal Year FY18 Q3*

April - June 2018	
Net Bill Issuance	(131)
Net Coupon Issuance	203
Subtotal: Net Marketable Borrowing	72
Ending Cash Balance	333
Beginning Cash Balance	290
Subtotal: Change in Cash Balance	43
Net Implied Funding for FY18 Q3**	29

US Total UST issuance YTD through 3 quarters of F18 has been $7.1 trillion, with $5.5 trillion of that in T-Bills (<1 year)!

(Source: Treasury, FFTT)

Security	April - June 2018 Bill Issuance			Fiscal Year-to-Date Bill Issuance		
	Gross	Maturing	Net	Gross	Maturing	Net
4-Week	550	670	(120)	1,770	1,755	15
13-Week	624	642	(18)	1,821	1,710	111
26-Week	546	477	69	1,587	1,341	246
52-Week	78	60	18	224	200	24
CMBs	0	80	(80)	139	179	(40)
Bill Subtotal	1,798	1,929	(131)	5,541	5,185	356

Security	April - June 2018 Coupon Issuance			Fiscal Year-to-Date Coupon Issuance		
	Gross	Maturing	Net	Gross	Maturing	Net
2-Year FRN	64	41	23	135	123	12
2-Year	95	78	17	253	156	97
3-Year	93	72	21	243	222	21
5-Year	106	90	16	311	345	(34)
7-Year	88	37	51	257	155	102
10-Year	68	12	56	196	52	144
30-Year	44	3	41	124	3	121
5-Year TIPS	16	53	(37)	30	53	(23)
10-Year TIPS	11	0	11	46	16	30
30-Year TIPS	5	0	5	17	0	17
Coupon Subtotal	590	387	203	1,612	1,125	487

	Gross	Maturing	Net	Gross	Maturing	Net
Total	2,388	2,316	72	7,153	6,310	843

*Privately-held marketable borrowing excludes rollovers (auction "add-ons") of Treasury securities held in the Federal Reserve's System Open Market Account (SOMA), but includes financing required due to SOMA redemptions.
**An end-of-June 2018 cash balance of $333 billion versus a beginning-of-April 2018 cash balance of $290 billion. By keeping the cash balance constant, Treasury arrives at the net implied funding number.

Mr. X: And what portion of the FX swaps being used to hedge USTs are less than one year in maturity?

Luke: Per the BIS, FX swaps with maturities of less than one year are the vast majority (more than 75 percent) of the total FX swaps outstanding.

[Mr. X looked at the chart on the next page that I sent before, continuing our conversation.]

Mr. X: So, tell me Luke, as a large percentage of both their FX swaps and their UST holdings mature over the next twelve months, why would an existing foreign private sector holder of USTs "roll" their UST holdings if the FX-hedged UST yield is currently nominally negative versus their own domestic bonds or other nations' bonds with positive yields?

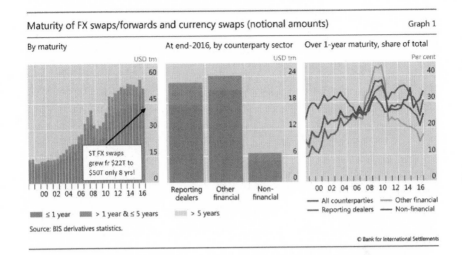

Maturity of FX swaps/forwards and currency swaps (notional amounts) — Graph 1

By maturity — At end-2016, by counterparty sector — Over 1-year maturity, share of total

ST FX swaps grew fr $22T to $50T only 8 yrs!

≤ 1 year   > 1 year & ≤ 5 years   > 5 years

All counterparties — Other financial
Reporting dealers — Non-financial

Source: BIS derivatives statistics.

© Bank for International Settlements

Luke: Oh…my…goodness. Some portion of foreign private sector investors will have no interest in rolling that $7-8 trillion given negative FX-hedged rates on USTs, and maybe a sizable portion, will they?

Mr. X: That would be my bet. Just out of curiosity, when you published the aforementioned report detailing the number of USTs the US needs to roll over in the next twelve months, how many of your clients thought that any portion of that $7-8 trillion would *not* get rolled, let alone possibly a sizable portion because foreign private sector buyers are unlikely to lock into negative rates on a hedged basis as their FX swaps and UST holdings mature?

Luke: None. Not one. Not even me.

Mr. X: I don't blame them—how could they know that cross-currency basis swaps were going to spike the way they have? Now do you see why I said "unless FX-hedged UST yields turn positive very soon, it may quickly represent a threat to US national security"?

Luke: Yes, I do. Do you think the US government realizes it?

Mr. X: I do.

Luke: Why?

Mr. X: Well, even if we were to assume they ignored what has now been a consistent series of "sloppy, tailing UST auctions" in recent weeks, there has been a more "qualitative" sign of US fiscal stress hiding in plain sight.

Luke: What do you mean?

Mr. X: When was the last time a US president (one with a penchant for being direct, no less) called the Fed "his biggest threat"? Why is Trump freezing Federal worker pay, and just this week, asking his cabinet members to cut their departments' budgets by 5 percent? Those headlines all strike me as odd things to do in the midst of what is widely-accepted by US investors as "a booming economy." Perhaps Trump's Treasury Secretary is telling him "all is not well" on the funding side…. I'll send you a few articles to back that up. [He emailed me the articles below.]

Trump says "Fed is his biggest threat" because it is raising rates too fast – 10/16/18

https://www.cnbc.com/2018/10/16/trump-says-fed-is-his-biggest-threat-because-it-is-raising-rates-too-fast.html

Trump to request 5% budget cut from all Cabinet members – 10/17/18

https://thehill.com/policy/finance/411860-trump-to-request-5-percent-cut-from-cabinet-members

Trump seeks to freeze pay in 2019 for Federal workers – 8/30/18

https://www.washingtonpost.com/politics/trump-seeks-to-freeze-pay-in-2019-for-federal-workers/2018/08/30/b00be5cc-ac78-11e8-a8d7-0f63ab8b1370_story.html?noredirect=on&utm_term=.9362a96d2b0a

Luke: I agree. Let's go back to Dizard's *Financial Times* article for a moment. Which banks are "cutting back on FX swaps exposure"? Does the article say?

Mr. X: I don't know for sure, but Credit Suisse's Zoltan Poszar, who is arguably one of the premier experts on the plumbing of the global financial system, wrote a report in November 2016 that suggested it is heavily comprised of big American banks. Let me read you a bit of it. [Source: Zoltan Poszar, Credit Suisse, "Global Money Notes #8", November 18, 2016].

> The end-state of the system is one where foreign banks raise their marginal dollars mostly in the FX swap market (from American banks) or the capital market (from asset managers).

> The end-state is dominated by American banks because post-reform, they are the only ones left with access to cheap retail dollars onshore to lend offshore via FX swaps—all foreign banks that used to lend via FX swaps raised dollars wholesale from prime funds (for a review of the impact of money fund reform on the FX swap market....

> As large American banks grow to dominate the FX swap market, they will inevitably become the marginal price setters in the system. Going forward, the key questions from a pricing perspective will be how American banks' growing FX swap books will push up against their balance sheet constraints: (1) how much balance sheet they will have to onboard these trades from an SLR perspective; (2) what will these trades do to their LCR; (3) what will the looming requirement to currency-match HQLA portfolios mean for their appetite to do these trades; and (4) will the Volcker Rule let them run speculative books?

None of these constraints mean anything good for the marginal cost of Eurodollar funding going forward, which means that what's referred to as a "global dollar shortage" is bound to get worse in the future. But in light of the points raised above, none of this is about a shortage of dollars per se, but rather a shortage of balance sheet to intermediate dollars (please, let's forget the whole "shortage versus scarcity" debate and call a spade a spade).

Luke: So, how do you think this is going to play out?

Mr. X: I think the answer to your question has three parts. First, given that the US has $7-8 trillion in USTs it needs to roll in the next twelve months, some portion of which foreign investors may *not* be interested in rolling at current cross-currency basis swap levels, I would say it is likely going to play out surprisingly quickly, because $7-8 trillion is just an enormous sum of money.

Secondly, I think UST auctions may get surprisingly sloppy for that same reason, putting pressure on the US economy, and possibly on risk assets in the very near term.

Thirdly, ultimately the urgency of my first and second points provide valuable context to this passage from Poszar's November 2016 report, paying particular attention to the final paragraph below. [He read to me, emphasizing the key points as he did so.]

> *The U.S.'s exorbitant privilege—its ability to borrow in its own currency anywhere in the world thanks to a vast and deep Eurodollar market—is waning. The first throw of sand at the gears of the global Eurodollar market was the adoption of Basel III which imposed liquidity requirements on a system born out of banks' desire to avoid reserve requirements in the first place.*
>
> *Basel III and money fund reform are turning the exorbitant privilege into an existential trilemma that's usually a*

problem for EM central banks with pegs to the dollar, rather than the Fed at the center of the dollar-based financial order.

According to the Fed's newfound trilemma, it is impossible to have constraints on bank balance sheets (restraining capital mobility in global money markets), a par exchange rate between onshore dollars and Eurodollars, and a domestically oriented monetary policy mandate. Something will have to give.

It's either the cross-currency basis, the foreign exchange value of the dollar or the hiking cycle.

Mr. X: The Fed is likely going to need to supply USD liquidity or pause Quantitative Tightening (QT), far sooner than most currently believe, in response to either sloppy UST auctions or a sell-off in risk assets or both. In other words, a major injection of USD liquidity is going to be needed from the Fed, ASAP.

Luke: Is it fair to say that the scenario Ray Dalio laid out on Bloomberg TV a little over a month ago—one that he said would occur about two years from now—might happen much sooner unless something changes very soon with cross-currency basis swaps to incentivize foreign private sector investors to continue rolling the $7-8 trillion in USTs that need rolling in the next twelve months?

Mr. X: Yes, I think that's fair; in fact, as I reread what Dalio said, it's probably more than fair. What Dalio laid out is pretty much exactly what could happen unless the USD is weakened one way or another, soon. Let me read it to you:

Ray Dalio, the billionaire hedge fund manager who founded Bridgewater Associates, effectively spelled out what doomsday looks like for the U.S. on live television. In an interview with Bloomberg TV on Wednesday, Dalio expressed his concern about two years from now, when, in his view, the economic recovery is likely to sputter out. It won't just be a debt problem this time around, he said, but rather a story about unfunded pension and health-care obligations. To address that looming crisis, the U.S. will need to ramp up issuance of U.S. Treasuries. And that's where it all unravels.

"We have to sell a lot of Treasury bonds, and we as Americans won't be able to buy all those Treasury bonds," Dalio said. That means foreign investors will have to step up. And they probably would, as long as the dollar remains strong. Otherwise, Treasury's dollar-denominated interest payments to buyers in China, Europe and Japan will be worth less and less.

But, to Dalio, that's not going to happen.

"The Federal Reserve at that point will have to print more money to make up for the deficit, have to monetize more and that'll cause a depreciation in the value of the dollar," he said. Pressed by interviewer Erik Schatzker, he said, "You easily could have a 30 percent depreciation in the dollar through that period of time." For context, the Bloomberg Dollar Spot Index fell 8.5 percent in 2017, and that was considered massive.

It all leads up to this critique of how the U.S. has gone on a borrowing binge in recent years. Remember, the $15.3 trillion Treasury market was the $4.9 trillion Treasury market a decade ago.

"We have the privileged position of being able to borrow in our own currency because we have the world's leading reserve currency. We are risking that by our finances—in other words, borrowing too much."

"Bridgewater Founder Ray Dalio Spells Out America's Worst Nightmare" – 9/12/18

https://www.bloomberg.com/view/articles/2018-09-12/ray-dalio-spells-out-america-s-worst-nightmare

Mr. X: I'd also add that Secretary of the Treasury Jack Lew's Congressional testimony around the debt ceiling about what happens if it gets harder for the US to roll USTs might be instructive to re-highlight. [Mr. X read the following to me.]

> In testimony before the Senate Finance Committee in October 2013, Lew explained why he wanted the Congress to agree to increase the federal debt limit—and why the Treasury has no choice but to constantly issue new debt. "Every week we roll over approximately $100 billion in U.S. bills," Lew told the committee. "If U.S. bondholders decided that they wanted to be repaid rather than continuing to roll over their investments, we could unexpectedly dissipate our entire cash balance." "There is no plan other than raising the debt limit that permits us to meet all of our obligations," Lew said. "Let me remind everyone," Lew said, "principal on the debt is not something we pay out of our cash flow of revenues. Principal on the debt is something that is a function of the markets rolling over."
>
> #### Transcript of Jack Lew's testimony on debt ceiling – *Washington Post*, 10/10/13
>
> https://www.washingtonpost.com/politics/running-transcript-jack-lews-testimony-on-debt-ceiling/2013/10/10/3edc0122-31b0-11e3-9c68-1cf643210300_story.html?utm_term=.2c6cdaa64f8d

Luke: Why don't we stop there. Thanks again for reaching out, Mr. X. I think the next several months are setting themselves up to be quite eventful indeed.

Mr. X: I agree. Let's talk again soon.

Chapter 9

VOLCKER'S "HELL OF A MESS IN EVERY DIRECTION" COMMENT MAY HINT AT BIGGEST MACRO RULE CHANGE IN FORTY-SEVEN YEARS

NOVEMBER 8, 2018

Four weeks after we met in early October, I let Mr. X know I would be back in Manhattan for meetings, and he asked if I would be able to have dinner and catch a flight home the following day, noting "There is much to discuss." Naturally, I obliged. On November 8, we met up for dinner in midtown Manhattan.

Luke: Thank you for joining me again, Mr. X. It is great to see you again.

Mr. X: You're welcome. It's always a pleasure to see you, Luke.

Luke: What's on your mind these days?

Mr. X: Did you see what former Fed Chairman Paul Volcker said last week?

Luke: No—what did he say?

Mr. X: He said, "The US is in a hell of a mess in every direction."

Luke: Do you agree with him?

Mr. X: I tend to agree with Volcker. I want to explain to you how we got to this point and Volcker's role in it because I believe Volcker's comment may carry significant informational value for investors.

Luke: How so?

Mr. X: Well, as you've noted in recent FFTTs, it appears trends are reaching a critical juncture. I've always found that it is helpful to understand how we got where we are to better understand where we may be going. Let's start at the beginning, or at least what will serve as the beginning for our purposes. [He handed me a sheet of paper that said the following.]

> "...the 1960s saw a growing disequilibrium in international payments, consequent on the deficit in the US balance of payments. The dollar became overvalued and the US found it increasingly difficult to meet its obligations to convert the dollar (into gold.) It is my firm conviction that a devaluation of the dollar combined with a substantial increase in the price of gold (as provided for in Article IV of the then Articles of Agreement of the International Monetary Fund) would have meant a real improvement of the situation.

– BIS Chair Jelle Zijlstra, 1981

Mr. X: In the time described in this quote, the US was running balance of payments deficits because of President Johnson's "Guns and Butter" programs. Zijlstra (a Dutch banker who demanded gold back from the US in the late 1960s and who went on to be the head of the BIS) believed the best solution to balancing US deficits in the late 1960s would have been a devaluation of the USD.

[He handed me another piece of paper.] Of course, as former Greek Finance Minister Yanis Varoufakis describes on this sheet of paper, the US had other ideas. Paul Volcker came up with a brilliant plan: If the US couldn't handle its *own* surpluses anymore, the US would structure a system that allowed it to handle *other* countries' surpluses:

> What did the Americans do when they realized that they had a deficit situation that was now actually growing? They did something absolutely astonishingly remarkable: They decided that the solution to the deficit problem was to enhance their deficits…to make them grow, and to make them grow at an increasing rate. Now that is an astonishing conception. How am I backing up this story?

> Well, Paul Volcker as a young man worked for Henry Kissinger before Kissinger became the foreign minister, Secretary of State for the United States (when he was still National Security Advisor). Volcker was working for him. Kissinger asked Volcker, who was a young banker, to come up with an idea as to how could American hegemony be expanded when the deficit is increasing. Volcker wrote a three-page report, which actually I have read. It was very difficult to get. You could not find it anywhere, even on the internet. I have it in a manuscript form and it was given to me by a friend, an American, some time ago; it is perhaps the most remarkable statement of the 20th century. Well, I am exaggerating, but you know what I mean.

> In it, Volcker said, well, if we can't remain hegemonic—that was the word he used—no, that is not a left-wing text, Volcker. If we can't remain hegemonic by—"handling" was the word he used—our surpluses, we should do it by handling other people's surpluses. And that's the Global Minotaur. Effectively what America did was this: We don't have a surplus anymore and so we can't recycle it. But we can recycle everybody else's surpluses and retain our hegemonic position through that.

And it is the very first time in human economic history or history in general that an empire is expanding its realm and its power and its strength and vitality by expanding its deficits. Usually when an empire has a deficit, it is the beginning of its decline. Not in the case of the United States.

Former Greek Finance Minister Yanis Varoufakis on the Volcker Study Group plan, 2014

https://www.youtube.com/watch?v=v62tw6ZdE28

Mr. X: While Volcker's plan was a masterstroke for certain interests in the US (the US government and US finance sectors in particular), other parts of the world were less sanguine about Volcker's plan.

For example, here's what a man once called "the most powerful bureaucrat in Brussels" and "the true leader of the EU," Martin Selmayr, wrote about what was transpiring around the time of Volcker's move. [He passed me a printed copy of the tweet.]

Martin Selmayr ✅
@MartinSelmayr

On 15/8/1971 Pdt Nixon used TV (a new medium at the time) to unilaterally end US commitment to the BrettonWoods system. Europe had to react, started work on a Monetary Union which eventually led to the €. Europe needs to take its destiny in its own hands.

Nixon Ends Bretton Woods International Monetary System
www.youtube.com

6:53 AM · Jun 10, 2018

235 Retweets   **377** Likes

Mr. X: The Europeans apparently didn't like Volcker's plan because, according to Selmayr, they "started work on a Monetary Union which eventually led to the EUR." Guess what happened once the EUR was launched?

Luke: I don't know. What?

Mr. X: The EU largely stopped buying USTs (stopped sterilizing US deficits). This was a problem for the US government:

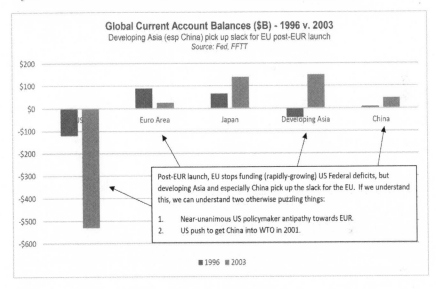

Luke: So what did this mean? What can we conclude from these moves?

Mr. X: The conclusions are clear: *After the EUR was launched in 1999, the EU largely stopped sterilizing US deficits.* This move by the EU was eerily reminiscent of something the EU had done thirty years prior. [He quoted, emphasizing key points, as follows.]

> One expert noted: *"The European financiers are forcing peace on us. For the first time in American history, our European creditors have forced the resignation of an American President."* (*Wall Street Journal*, April 4, 1968).

Until 1968, Europe had, in an important respect, borne the major cost of supporting world confidence that America's overseas military expenditures would not impair the value of America's currency. *Europe did this by holding on to the dollars thrown off by these expenditures rather than cashing them in for US gold.* The Europeans had protested since 1964 against absorbing these dollars, and finally, with the gold crisis, they drew the line against continuing thus to finance US military policy.

America was left to pay the costs itself, but they were beyond its means. And at that point it became clear that the US could not continue its current rate of overseas military spending—much less increase it—without bringing on a complete collapse of confidence in its currency.

"Sieve of Gold," *Rampart Magazine*, May 1968

http://www.gata.org/files/RampartsMay1968-SieveOfGold.pdf

However, unlike when the EU stopped sterilizing US deficits in 1968, when the EU did so post-1999 EUR launch, the US government was able to find a new "sugar daddy": **China**. China entered the World Trade Organization in late 2001 (below), and Chinese recycling/sterilization of US deficits promptly went into hyperdrive, as Chinese holdings of USTs rose from $60B in 2001 to $1.3T by 2011. [Mr. X handed me the following chart.]

China formally enters WTO – 12/11/01

https://www.wsj.com/articles/SB1008010719257340800

The ratio of the annual increase in Chinese UST holdings divided by the annual increase in the US Federal deficit from 2002-2011 yields an interesting conclusion: China effectively funded 10-50 percent of US deficits for a decade. [He handed me the next chart.]:

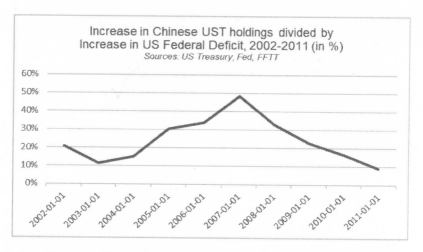

Luke: It seems like something began to change at some point.

Mr. X: Indeed…something began changing in 2012-13. Perhaps it was how the US was increasingly using the USD as a weapon (sanctioning Iran out of the SWIFT system in 2012, threatening to kick Russia out of the SWIFT system in 2013 and again in 2014). Perhaps it was the surprising announcement of renewed Fed quantitative easing in 2012, but regardless, in late 2013, China announced it would no longer increase its holdings of USTs… [Mr. X passed me copies of the several following charts and their sources.]

PBOC: No longer in China's favor to boost record FX reserves (stockpile USTs) – 11/20/13

https://www.bloomberg.com/news/articles/2013-11-20/pboc-says-no-longer-in-china-s-favor-to-boost-record-reserves

…and then followed through on that announcement:

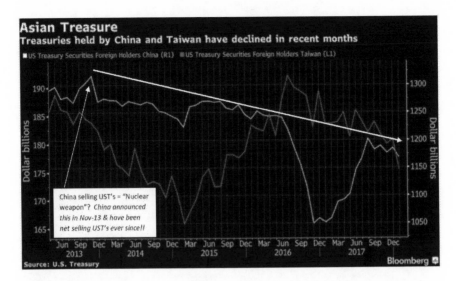

Asian Treasure
Treasuries held by China and Taiwan have declined in recent months

China selling UST's = "Nuclear weapon"? *China announced this in Nov-13 & have been net selling UST's ever since!!*

Source: U.S. Treasury

China's effectively joining the EU by ceasing to sufficiently grow UST holdings created an existential problem for the system Volcker had recommended all the way back in the early 1970s: There were two big surplus regions in the world, and neither one was growing USTs holdings anymore! *The scenario Zijlstra warned about on the front page had become reality:*

> "…the 2nd Oil Crisis could be worked through, slowly, but the international financial system could not survive a 3rd Oil Crisis—the inflation would make it impossible to recycle the petrodollars to the oil importing countries with any hope of repayment, trade would crumble, and the system would be brought to its knees." – **BIS Chair Jelle Zijlstra, 1980**

Luke, as you've noted before, shortly after China stopped growing UST stockpiles, the US created a patchwork of demand for USTs, first regulating US banks into buying more USTs via "High Quality Liquid Asset (HQLA)" regulations…

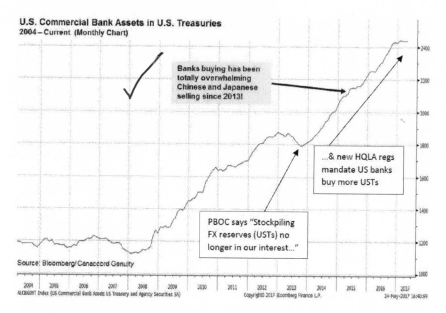

U.S. Commercial Bank Assets in U.S. Treasuries
2004 – Current (Monthly Chart)

Banks buying has been totally overwhelming Chinese and Japanese selling since 2013!

...& new HQLA regs mandate US banks buy more USTs

PBOC says "Stockpiling FX reserves (USTs) no longer in our interest..."

Source: Bloomberg/ Canaccord Genuity

...and then regulating US money market funds into buying more USTs via MMF Reforms....

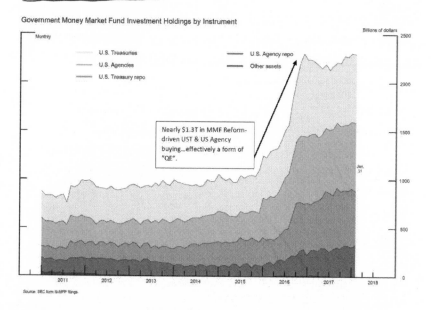

Government Money Market Fund Investment Holdings by Instrument

Billions of dollars

Monthly

U.S. Treasuries
U.S. Agencies
U.S. Treasury repo
U.S. Agency repo
Other assets

Nearly $1.3T in MMF Reform-driven UST & US Agency buying...effectively a form of "QE".

Source: SEC form N-MFP filings.

...and most recently, regulating/encouraging US corporations to repatriate USDs and buy more USTs...

Tax Reform wrinkle is encouraging corporate pensions to buy USTs – *WSJ*, 7/5/18

https://www.wsj.com/articles/the-tax-wrinkle-that-is-making-pension-funds-buy-more-treasurys-1530783000

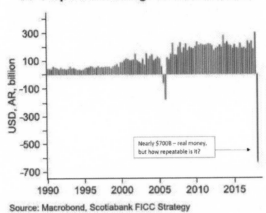

US Corporate Earnings Retained Abroad

Nearly $700B – real money, but how repeatable is it?

Source: Macrobond, Scotiabank FICC Strategy

Luke: Yes, we've written about this a number of times—these dynamics were eerily similar to Emerging Markets regulating the domestic sector into financing the government once external sources of financing were lost.

Mr. X: Yes, and you've been one of the few to make that equivalence, which I think is quite accurate. Importantly, in addition to regulating the domestic private sector into buying USTs, the US government was at the same time implementing healthcare reforms (ACA) that pushed a greater share of US healthcare costs onto US consumers.

The problem was that with the US effectively funding its own deficits for the first time in seventy years, US domestic consumption began being "crowded out" by US government deficits, driving slower US growth.

Ironically then, the first symptom of China joining the EU in ceasing to grow UST holdings can be seen below: The initial reaction was not *rising* ten-year UST yields, but rather *falling* ten-year UST yields because consumer spending slowed as US consumers had to deal with rising healthcare out-of-pocket costs, rising short-term interest rates, and a rising USD. [He passed me the next chart.]

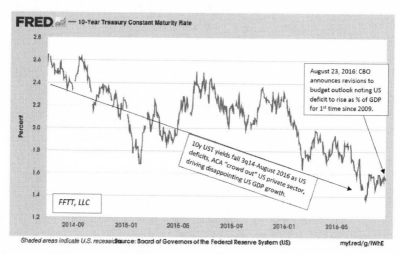

Mr. X: Besides slowing the US economy, US efforts to reduce US deficits and fund those deficits internally for the first time in seventy years worked well...until the third quarter of 2016, when the post-third quarter of 2014 crowding out of the US private sector drove the first widening of the US deficit as a percentage of the GDP since 2009. This was the first key tipping point. In plain English, US attempts to finance its own deficit for the first time in seventy years were now resulting in a widening of the US deficit! This was a "Greece problem with US characteristics." [Mr. X passed me the next chart that illustrated his point.]

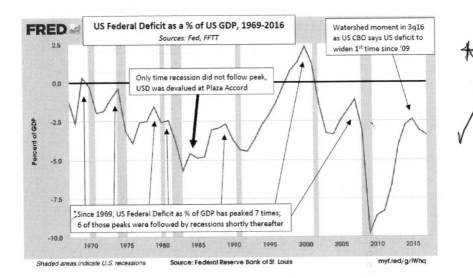

Interestingly, once US efforts to reduce deficits began driving wider deficits, the ten-year UST market seems to have begun sensing it almost immediately. Since the third quarter of 2016, ten-year UST yields have generally risen.

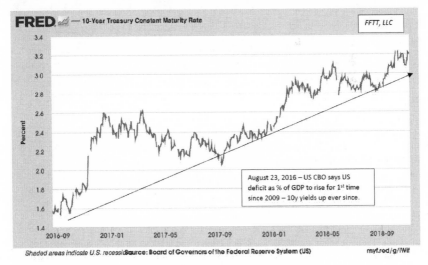

The third quarter of 2016 was the first major tipping point in the process of US deficits mattering for the first time in seventy years. In my view, the next major tipping point in this process came earlier this year, and it is shown in this chart. [He passed me the chart below.] USTs began selling off in major equity market risk-offs in 2018 in the most sustained manner we've seen in at least twenty years....

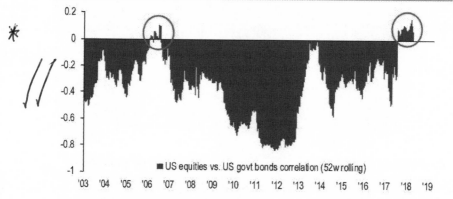

Chart 3: Positive correlation between SPY & TLT since Feb'18

Source: BofA Merrill Lynch Global Investment Strategy, Bloomberg

Additionally, around the same time that UST yields began rising in equity sell-offs, another signal of USD-centric system stress emerged: Gold and inverted US real rates diverged in the most sustained manner since late 2004 to early 2005. [He handed me yet another chart. He had obviously come well-prepared for our discussion.]

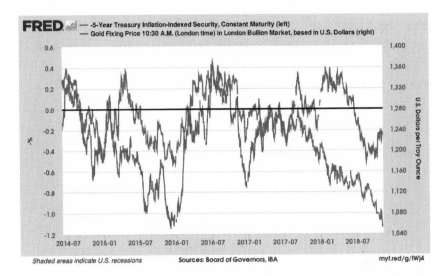

FRED — -5-Year Treasury Inflation-Indexed Security, Constant Maturity (left)
— Gold Fixing Price 10:30 A.M. (London time) in London Bullion Market, based in U.S. Dollars (right)

Shaded areas indicate U.S. recessions   Sources: Board of Governors, IBA   myf.red/g/lWj4

With the preceding context, the "hell of a mess in every direction" that Volcker refers to becomes clearer: The two biggest surplus countries (Germany and China) are no longer recycling their surpluses into USTs.

Luke: To use your phrase, the US needs a new "sugar daddy" to sterilize US government deficits, doesn't it?

Mr. X: (smiling) Yes, the US needs a new "sugar daddy"—but using the "China financing 10-50% of US deficits from 2002-11" as a guide, this implies another nation running $100-$500B/year in surpluses with the US in coming years—$100-$500B per year is 10-50 percent of $1T deficits projected by US Congressional Budget Office (CBO).

Who is going to do that? India? Unlikely. Africa? Possible…but this would require either massive price inflation of African commodity exports to the US or the offshoring of the US manufacturing base to Africa. The problem with the latter solution, of course, is that a quorum of the US' manufacturing base already resides in China.

What commodities can Africa export to the US at inflated-enough prices that would drive $100-500B per year of surpluses to fund UST buying? Could African commodities be inflated that much without crashing the global economy as EMs find themselves unable to afford African commodity imports? The answer to both questions is unclear to me.

Luke: So, what does this imply?

Mr. X: What this, in turn, suggests is that the US is once again back in a similar position to the one it found itself in after the launch of the EUR in 1999 when the EU stopped recycling surpluses into USTs...except the US is running a massive deficit now (versus a surplus then), US demographics are much older today, big chunks of the US' manufacturing base have already been offshored to China, and there is no clear region we can run big enough surpluses with to fund future US deficits.

This chart provides a guide of what happened to commodities, and by extension, the USD the last two times the US found itself in this situation. [Mr. X handed me the chart below.]

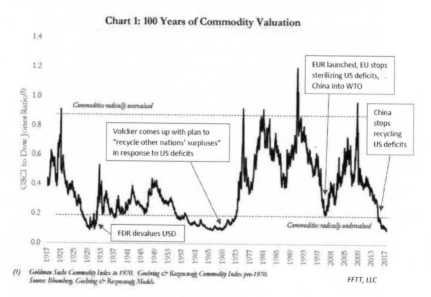

Chart 1: 100 Years of Commodity Valuation

(1) Goldman Sachs Commodity Index to 1970. Goehring & Rozencwajg Commodity Index pre-1970.
Source: Bloomberg, Goehring & Rozencwajg Models.

FFTT, LLC

Luke: So, what is your conclusion for all of this?

Mr. X: The conclusion is we appear to be in a similar spot to where we were in 1970 and 1999…commodities at/near 100-year lows relative to financial assets and the USD at/near recent highs…except this time we have worse demographics, a worse deficit position, a worse debt position, and no obvious successor to be our next deficit-recycling "sugar daddy."

This, in my view, is likely why Volcker said the US is in "a hell of a mess in every direction." If this is the case, what is the release valve? For an answer to that, we must go "back to the future," to the period when the US first ran into deficit trouble, but before Volcker proposed recycling other nations' surpluses since we know there are no immediate "other surpluses" to recycle. In 1981, BIS Chair Jelle Zijlstra said:

> the 1960s saw a growing disequilibrium in international payments, consequent on the deficit in the US balance of payments. The dollar became overvalued and the US found it increasingly difficult to meet its obligations to convert the dollar (into gold.) It is my firm conviction that a devaluation of the dollar combined with a substantial increase in the price of gold (as provided for in Article IV of the then Articles of Agreement of the International Monetary Fund) would have meant a real improvement of the situation.

In plain English: When the US was faced with this problem in the early 1970s, we had two choices:

1. Devalue the USD.

2. Find another nation/region that was running surpluses that we could "handle," as Varoufakis described.

As Varoufakis noted in the quote I handed you earlier, in the early 1970s, the US chose option #2. This drove a series of outcomes, the most pronounced of which was that US government and US finance sectors benefited to the detriment of US production/manufacturing assets. The system Volcker created faced its first test in 1999 when the EUR was launched, which effectively allowed German surpluses to be recycled into Southern Europe instead of into USTs. This system received a new but temporary lease on life when China went into the WTO, as I noted earlier.

However, once China stopped recycling surpluses into USTs nearly five years ago, the system faced the same test, except from a much worse starting point. This implies the US needs to do one of two things, ASAP:

1. Find a new country/region running large surpluses that we can "handle."

2. Get the EU to break up so that Germany will be able to recycle US surpluses once again.

However, if the US cannot do one of those two things very soon, there is only one release valve: The USD, as the Fed is forced to become the US' new "sugar daddy," and far sooner than most think. The fact that FX-hedged UST yields went nominally-negative in late September has introduced a sense of urgency to the decision tree I shared earlier, as hinted at by these two articles from this week. [He passed to me the following.]

30y UST bond auction draws weakest demand in nearly a decade – *WSJ*, 11/8/18

https://www.wsj.com/articles/treasury-bond-auction-draws-weakest-demand-in-nearly-a-decade-1541629316

> Investors & dealers submitted bids totaling 2.06 times the amount of debt sold at Wednesday's auction. This multiple, known as the bid-to-cover ratio, was the lowest for a 30-yr bond auction since February 2009

Investors shy away from 3y UST auction, bid-to-cover 2nd lowest since 2009 – *FT*, 11/5/18

https://www.ft.com/content/f3f56754-e12a-11e8-8e70-5e22a430c1ad

> Investors backed away from today's $37bn sale of three-year Treasuries, as the potential for volatility stemming from tomorrow's US elections, alongside the bumper supply coming to market this week, appeared to sap demand.

> The bid-to-cover ratio, an indication of the number of investors who put in offers to buy the debt, dropped to its second lowest level for a three-year auction since 2009.

Luke: So, in your opinion, what is the most likely outcome; what will the US choose?

Mr. X: In my opinion, the most likely outcome is that the Fed will be forced to become the US' new "sugar daddy," effectively becoming the financier of last resort, and eventually financier of first resort for US government deficits.

Luke: What does that mean in plain English?

Mr. X: What it means in plain English is that I think it is highly likely we will see the Fed's balance sheet begin to expand aggressively at some point in 2019.

Luke: Wow...not many people think that's likely to happen as we sit here today.

Mr. X: I think it's all but inevitable.

Luke: Why don't we stop there for today?

Mr. X: Sounds good. Thanks again for meeting with me.

Chapter 10

IF BIG DEFICITS + TIGHTER MONETARY POLICY = USD+, THEN BIG DEFICITS + LOOSER MONETARY POLICY = _____?

DECEMBER 13, 2018

My phone rang; it was a foreign area code—Mr. X was calling. It was a testament to how fast events were happening that calls that used to happen once or twice every six months now seemed to be coming monthly.

"Mr. X," I answered, "great to hear from you. What's going on?"

"Do you think you could get to Chicago on short notice? I'll be there tomorrow night."

"Happy to," I replied, knowing there are many flights to Chicago out of Cleveland daily. "Where are you staying?"

I wrote down Mr. X's hotel in downtown Chicago and made my flight arrangements. Thirty hours later, I found myself shaking hands with Mr. X in the lobby of The Ritz-Carlton, Chicago.

Luke: Mr. X, it is great to talk to you again. What is catching your attention these days?

Mr. X: What's catching my attention is that the "Soros/Druckenmiller-inspired strong USD playbook" you and I discussed nearly two years ago and which was tried by the US Administration and US Fed over the past nine months just failed, but the USD bulls are as yet still in denial about it. [Mr. X handed me the following transcript from our January 17, 2017 conversation and we both took a few minutes to read it. It follows below.]

> **Mr. X:** There seems to be a Soros/Druckenmiller-inspired trade being put on around the world that says that the US can run the same playbook it ran in 1980 or the same playbook that Germany ran in 1989.

Luke: What does that "Soros/Druckenmiller playbook" say?

Mr. X: It says the US can run increasing deficits and simultaneously raise rates (loosen fiscal policy, tighten monetary policy), and in so doing, drive a stronger USD:

> > Druckenmiller: "I never had more conviction about any trade than I did about the long side of the Deutsche mark when the Berlin Wall came down. One of the reasons I was so bullish on the Deutsche mark was a radical currency theory proposed by George Soros in his book, *The Alchemy of Finance*. His theory was that if a huge deficit were accompanied by an expansionary fiscal policy and tight monetary policy, the country's currency would actually rise. The dollar provided a perfect test case in the 1981-84 period. At the time, the general consensus was that the dollar would decline because of the huge budget deficit. However, because money was attracted into the country by a tight

monetary policy, the dollar actually went sharply higher.

"When the Berlin Wall came down, it was one of those situations that I could see as clear as day. West Germany was about to run up a huge budget deficit to finance the rebuilding of East Germany. At the same time, the Bundesbank was not going to tolerate any inflation. I went headlong into the Deutsche mark. It turned out to be a terrific trade." Source: *The New Market Wizards* by Jack Schwager

Luke: What is the problem with that playbook, in your opinion?

Mr. X: The short version is this: The degree of debt and financialization in the US economy are so great that the tighter monetary policy required to strengthen the USD will likely blow up the US economy before fiscal stimulus benefits accrue, forcing US deficits to widen from collapsing tax revenues instead of from accelerating productive fiscal deficits.

The longer version of the problems with that playbook? The differences now versus then are myriad:

1. The US and German Federal deficit levels in both of those cases versus the US now.
2. US and German manufacturing bases then, versus the US' manufacturing base now.
3. US financialization now versus then.
4. US interest rates derivatives now versus then.
5. The reserve status of the USD now versus then (and the $9T in offshore USD debt that reserve status has driven.)

Now, to be clear, the US could certainly *attempt* to run the playbook above that it ran in 1980 and Germany ran in

1989, but in my opinion, if the US tries, it will likely fail, and possibly fail disastrously.

Luke: Why?

Mr. X: Because US economic financialization levels mean US tax receipts will fall as rates rise—indeed, US tax receipts are already falling year over year, after only what? Two tiny interest rate hikes and a 100bp increase in LIBOR in twelve months?

As this occurs, it will lead to rising US funding needs, which with US Federal debt levels above 100 percent of GDP, higher rates, and a continued foreign official creditor UST buyers' strike, could kick off a US BoP crisis.

Again, to be clear, I'm not saying the US will not attempt to run the "Druckenmiller/Soros" playbook of loosening fiscal stimulus while simultaneously tightening monetary policy, or that such an action wouldn't drive the USD higher in the near term; it likely would were it attempted. What I'm saying is that as Hugo Salinas-Price noted, further moves to strengthen the USD will force other nations to move away from the USD at an even faster rate than they already are.

Ultimately, the differences I highlighted earlier of now versus 1980 US or 1989 Germany suggest the end game must be a USD devaluation.

Luke: While we did not get the USD devaluation we discussed in January 2017, we did get the biggest decline in the USD in decades in 2017, down 12 percent, when virtually everyone thought the USD would rise in 2017.

Mr. X: Yes. The US Administration did not run the "Druckenmiller strong USD playbook" in 2017. For whatever reason, it waited to run it until earlier this year, beginning around late February or early March, as the Fed changed its tone on rate hikes while the US government passed US Tax Reforms that increased US deficits. Crucially, from March until September of this year, the USD responded exactly as Druckenmiller described in *Market Wizards*…but the "Druckenmiller strong USD" playbook began failing in October.

Luke: Why do you say that?

Mr. X: Because exactly what we said would happen if the "Druckenmiller strong USD playbook" was tried began to happen in October:

> The degree of debt and financialization in the US economy are so great that the tighter monetary policy required to strengthen the USD will likely blow-up the US economy before fiscal stimulus benefits accrue, forcing US deficits to widen from collapsing tax revenues instead of from accelerating productive fiscal deficits.

Luke: What areas of the "indebted and financialized US economy" are you speaking of that are "blowing up"?

Mr. X: Pretty much all of it… [He listed a series of areas, producing a chart or article to back up each point.]

High yield debt…

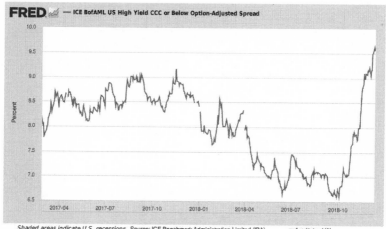

...and investment grade debt:

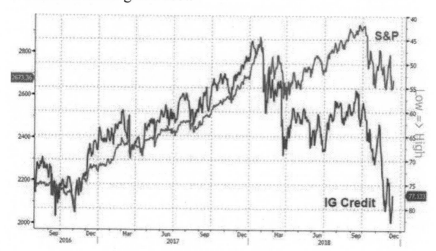

Source: Bloomberg, via Zero Hedge

US Equities…

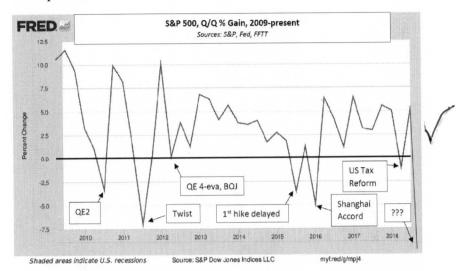

US residential construction…

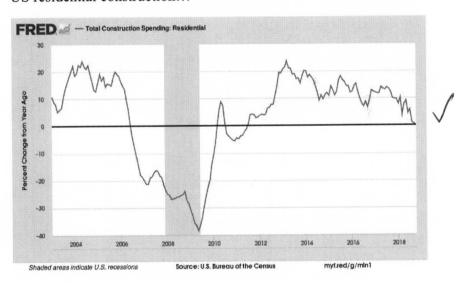

US Housing and Real Estate [below]...

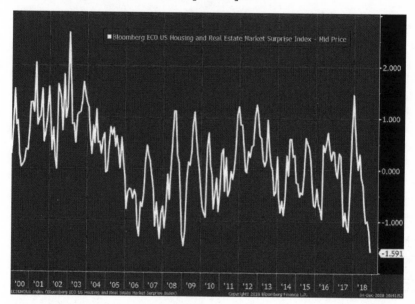

The US banking sector [below]:

**US banks haven't behaved like this since 2009 –
12/11/18**

> https://www.alhambrapartners.com/2018/12/11/us-banks-
> havent-behaved-like-this-since-2009/

The highly interest-rate-sensitive (and near-global, high-cost
producer) US shale and oil production sectors are back to near the
lows of early 2016 [XLE, top chart & XOP, bottom chart]...

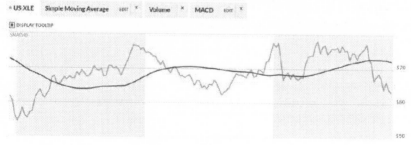

Source: StockCharts.com

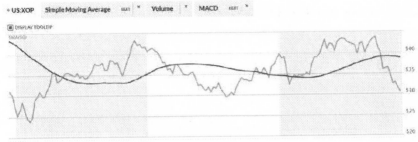

Source: StockCharts.com

...despite the fact that oil prices are still some 75 percent higher than they were at the lows of early 2016:

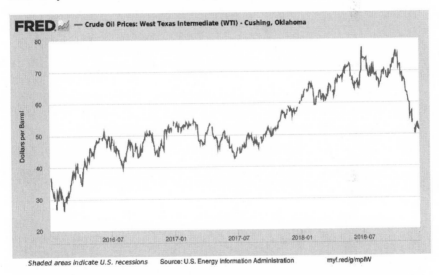

Unsurprisingly given all of the above, US initial unemployment claims have recently turned notably higher...

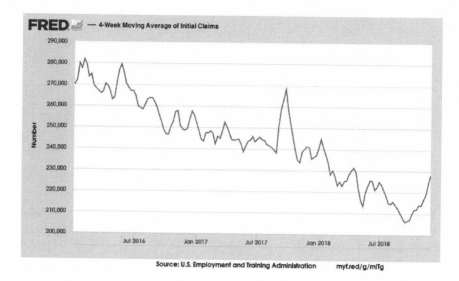

Source: U.S. Employment and Training Administration   myf.red/g/miTg

...as the overall US economy has slowed markedly, particularly post-September, as you can see in this ECRI chart [next page].

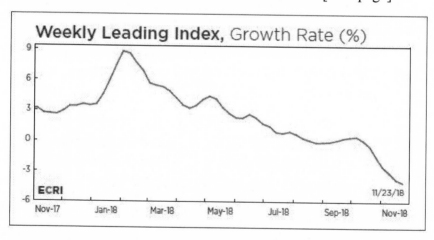

When taken together, what the prior series of charts show is that the financial markets that drive US consumption growth, US tax receipts, the financialized housing market, the financialized US energy production market—all of it—is now driving weakening US employment and GDP growth. As I said two years ago:

Now, to be clear, the US could certainly *attempt* to run the playbook above that it ran in 1980 and Germany ran in 1989, but in my opinion, if the US tries, it will likely fail, and possibly fail disastrously.

Luke: It looks like you were right—they finally did try it in March 2018, and now it is failing *spectacularly*.

Mr. X: Indeed.

Luke: You said before that the "Druckenmiller strong USD playbook" worked through September but then fell apart. What happened in October to cause it to fail so rapidly?

Mr. X: In my opinion, this was a crucial driver: FX-hedged UST yields went negative in late September. We talked about this back in October; this has, in turn, begun hurting foreign private sector demand for USTs [Mr. X handed me the following articles]:

Bond Traders Are Paid Big to Dump U.S. Treasuries and Go Abroad – 10/17/18

https://www.bloomberg.com/news/articles/2018-10-17/bond-traders-get-paid-big-to-dump-u-s-treasuries-and-go-abroad

> But more than just being a savvy trade idea, it underscores how *the longstanding and popular narrative of the U.S. as a go-to destination for yield-seeking bond investors is little more than an illusion.*
>
> While U.S. investors have few incentives to stay at home, the sky-high cost for foreigners to hedge the dollar means they have little cause to buy Treasuries. In some cases, their effective *yields* can fall below zero. Any letup in demand could drive up U.S. borrowing costs, at a time when the

government can ill-afford to lose investors as it raises ever more debt to meet its widening budget deficits. (Of course, bond investors can always opt not to hedge, though making a bet on the direction of currencies entails an added risk.)

Foreign investors spurn U.S. Treasuries as curve threatens to invert – 12/11/18

https://www.reuters.com/article/us-usa-bonds-foreigners/foreign-investors-spurn-us-treasuries-as-curve-threatens-to-invert-idUSKBN1OA0J6

> "…in the plan for next year, which we have just started contemplating, we will consider whether to flip back to JGBs from hedged foreign bonds, which we see as substitute for JGBs," he said.

Luke: What, in plain English, is the relevance of FX-hedged UST yields going negative per above to the "Druckenmiller strong USD playbook"?

Mr. X: It means the "Druckenmiller strong USD playbook" went from choking out the rest of the world to choking out the US and US markets.

Luke: Why?

Mr. X: Because the US began having to fund a much greater percentage of its own deficits, which it can do, but not with US equity markets priced anywhere near where they were at the end of September. The US' deficits went from crowding out the world to crowding out the US economy. As long as FX-hedged UST yields stay negative, US risk markets will likely remain under pressure. It's fascinating….

Luke: What's fascinating?

Mr. X: USD bulls are so focused on the first-order USD liquidity aspects that should drive the USD higher (all else equal) that they're ignoring the second-order impacts seen in the rapidly-slowing US economy and risk asset feedback, which, as we showed, has intensified markedly ever since FX-hedged UST yields went negative.

Luke: Why do you say they're ignoring the second-order impacts?

Mr. X: Look at speculative positioning on the USD in this chart:

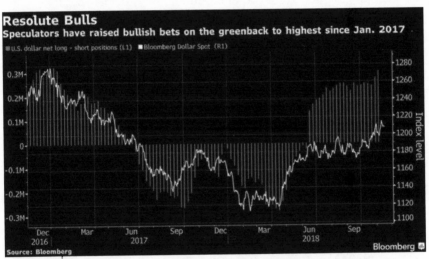

Luke: But the USD bulls have a point, don't they? I mean, negative FX-hedged UST yields just drains USD liquidity from the world even faster because we have to fund our own deficits, right? I mean, shouldn't this drive the USD higher and higher until something breaks?

Mr. X: Oh, sure…that's exactly what the USD liquidity implications of negative FX-hedged UST yields are, at least near-term. But that was my point before—the US economy *is* breaking. The USD bulls think the Fed is going to be willing to, as we called it seven months ago, "burn down the world"…but I don't think they'll do that. I think the easy money has been made in owning USDs. I think the USD will have to be weakened significantly and soon.

Luke: What if you're wrong?

Mr. X: As long as FX-hedged UST yields remain negative and the USD is not weakened meaningfully, the only assets you'll want to own are cash and gold. And if authorities let this situation persist for too long without weakening the USD, by the second half of next year, you may be getting a call from me to begin taking cash out of the bank and stockpiling essentials in your basement.

Luke: It's that serious?

Mr. X: It's that serious. In November 2016, the BIS said "there may be no winners from a stronger USD." They weren't kidding. What negative FX-hedged UST yields mean is that the USD is already way too strong, *now…today*.

Luke: So, what do you think could be the catalyst for a USD decline/weakening?

Mr. X: I think it could be either a US/China trade deal that could have a "Plaza Accord" type component that weakens the USD, or a US economic weakness that forces the Fed to first pause Quantitate Tightening (QT), then pause rate hikes, then cut rates, and finally, begin growing its balance sheet again.

Luke: You think the Fed could begin growing its balance sheet again?

Mr. X: If FX-hedged UST yields remain negative and the USD is not weakened soon, I think it's quite likely the Fed will be forced to begin growing its balance sheet no later than the fourth quarter of 2019, and quite possibly sooner. My guess is markets will begin sniffing out such a possibility by no later than the end of the first quarter to early in the second quarter of 2019.

Luke: Well, Mr. X, thank you for your thoughts. You've given me and my readers a lot to consider. Why don't we wrap it up for this session?

Mr. X: Sounds good. It is always a pleasure to talk to you. I look forward to speaking again with you soon. If I don't talk to you before then, have a great holiday and a Happy New Year.

Luke: You too, Mr. X.

Epilogue

"THE MOST IMPORTANT CHART TO CONSIDER FOR 2019"

JANUARY 3, 2019

On January 3, 2019, I found myself on a flight from Newark Airport to London Heathrow with my wife. Once we reached altitude, I opened up my laptop to check my email. A message from Mr. X hit my inbox with the subject line "The Most Important Chart to Consider for 2019?" I immediately opened Mr. X's email and read:

> Luke,
>
> I wanted to show you this chart, which I think is easily the most important chart to consider for 2019, given how weak 2018 finished and how 2019 has begun.

The S&P 500 was down more than 2 percent as I read Mr. X's email.

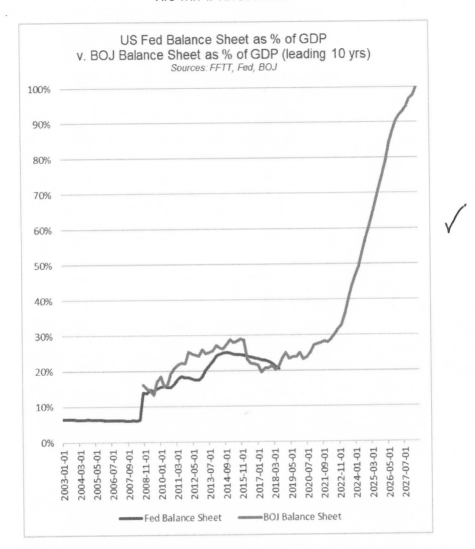

US Fed Balance Sheet as % of GDP
v. BOJ Balance Sheet as % of GDP (leading 10 yrs)
Sources: FFTT, Fed, BOJ

Below the chart, Mr. X had written:

Luke, after December's market selloff, I have been re-reading my notes from Liaquat Ahamed's book *Lords of Finance: The Bankers Who Broke the World*. It hit me that what the Fed is attempting to do has been attempted before—there is nothing new under the sun. Read these quotes:

There were essentially only 2 ways to restore the past balance between the value of gold reserves & the total money supply. One was to put the whole process of inflation into reverse & deflate the monetary bubble by actually contracting the amount of currency in circulation...but it was painful. It inescapably involved a period of dramatically tight credit & high interest rates. The alternative was to accept that past mistakes were now irreversible, & reestablish monetary balance with a sweep of the pen by reducing the value of the domestic currency in terms of gold (devalue.) The US & UK took the route of deflation; Germany & France that of devaluation/inflation.

> — **Liaquat Ahamed,** *Lords of Finance:*
> *The Bankers Who Broke the World,* **p. 156**

Here's how it played out last time:

By the end of 1922, the BOE had succeeded in bringing prices down by 50%, & the pound, which had fallen as low as $3.20 v. the gold-backed dollar, climbed back within 10% of pre-war parity of $4.86. But the number of unemployed in Britain would not fall below 1 million for the next 20 years [FFTT: Akin to ~10% US unemployment].

> — **Liaquat Ahamed,** *Lords of Finance:*
> *The Bankers Who Broke the World,* **p. 161**

Here's how it is playing out this time, using your transcript of our conversation we had in May of last year:

I am becoming increasingly fearful that the US is now deploying its "nuclear weapon of currency war. The US Fed & Treasury will essentially weaponize the USD to an increasingly extreme degree, essentially destroying the global economy in order to preserve the USD's role as main reserve currency. If this option is chosen, the bet they are making is that it will drive demand for USDs and USTs higher, breaking global EM markets and commodities first, followed shortly thereafter by the US economy and, ultimately, the US fiscal situation.

— Mr. X, 5/3/18

And here is my point in highlighting these quotes to you— in my opinion, here's the choice the Fed will likely face before the end of 2019E:

Von Havenstein faced a real dilemma. Were he to refuse to print the money necessary to finance the deficit, he risked causing a sharp rise in interest rates as the government scrambled to borrow from every source. The mass unemployment that would ensue, he believed, would bring on a domestic economic & political crisis, which in Germany's current fragile state might precipitate a real political convulsion. As the prominent Hamburg banker Max Warburg, a member of the Reichsbank's board of directors, put it, the dilemma was 'whether one wished to stop the inflation & trigger the revolution,' or continue to print money. Loyal servant of the state that he was, Von Havenstein had no wish to destroy the last vestiges of the old order.

— Liaquat Ahamed, *Lords of Finance:*
***The Bankers Who Broke the World*, p. 125**

Here's the context for the environment in which the Fed is operating:

The situation is worse than it was in 2007. Our macroeconomic ammunition to fight downturns is essentially all used up. It will become obvious in the next recession that many of these debts will never be serviced or repaid, & this will be uncomfortable for a lot of people who think they own assets that are worth something. The only question is whether we are able to look reality in the eye & face what is coming in an orderly fashion, or whether it will be disorderly. Debt jubilees have been going on for 5,000 years, as far back as the Sumerians.

— **William White, OECD, former chief economist of BIS, Jan 2016**

"Trigger the revolution or continue to print money"…"orderly or disorderly"…"it will become obvious in the next recession that many of these debts will never be serviced or repaid."

Luke, this is where we find ourselves today. I am struck by the still seemingly-cavalier attitudes of many newly-minted "liquidationalists" I have seen on CNBC and Twitter; they think the Fed should stand aside, do nothing, and "trigger the revolution."

Put me down—I think the Fed's balance sheet is likely to begin following the path of the Bank of Japan's balance sheet, much sooner than most investors think. My guess is this may be good for stock prices, but ultimately, it's really good for gold. I've begun buying a lot more gold, and gold miners as well.

Enjoy your trip to London; I wish I could meet you and your wife there. Let's talk when you return.

Best, Mr. X

As I looked at the chart and read the quotes Mr. X had emailed me, I said out loud, "Whoa." My wife looked at me and said, "What?"

"I just read a really provocative email from Mr. X. He's begun buying a lot more gold, and gold miners as well. I think 2019 is going to be a really interesting year."

THE END

ABOUT THE AUTHOR

Luke Gromen has twenty-five years of experience in equity research, equity research sales, and as a macro/thematic analyst. He is the founder and president of the macro/thematic research firm FFTT, LLC, which he founded in early 2014 to address and leverage the opportunity he saw created by applying what clients and former colleagues consistently described as a "unique ability to connect the dots" during a time when he saw an increasing "silo-ing" of perspectives occurring on Wall Street and in corporate America. FFTT caters to institutions and sophisticated individuals by aggregating a wide variety of macroeconomic, thematic, and sector trends in an unconventional manner to identify investable developing economic bottlenecks for his clients.

Prior to founding FFTT, Luke was a founding partner of Cleveland Research Company, where he worked from 2006-14. At CRC, Luke worked in sales and edited CRC's flagship weekly thematic research summary piece, *Straight from the Source*, for the firm's clients. Prior to that, Luke was a partner at Midwest Research, where he worked in equity research and sales from 1996-2006. While in sales, Luke was a founding editor of Midwest's widely-read weekly thematic summary, *Heard in the Midwest*, for the firm's clients, in which he aggregated and combined proprietary research from *Midwest* with inputs from other sources.

Luke Gromen holds a BBA in Finance and Accounting from the University of Cincinnati and received his MBA from Case Western Reserve University. He earned the CFA designation in 2003

GET INSIDE THE RING

SUBSCRIBE TO FFTT TREE RINGS

For more information about subscription options to FFTT investment research, please visit:
www.FFTT-LLC.com

AUGUST 7, 2020

FFTT, LLC
the forest for the trees

FFTT "Tree Rings": *The 10 Most Interesting Things We've Read Recently*

Here are this week's "Tree Rings". Have a great weekend! LG

1. *"US will borrow estimated $2 trillion in 2H20, US Treasury says"* (page 2)

2. *"Without significant stimulus, we est. 35-45% of 30m small biz's in the US will begin to permanently close by Labor Day"* (page 4)

3. *"NY Governor Cuomo begs wealthy New Yorkers to come home to save ailing city"* (page 6)

4. Right on cue: *"Fed's Brainard lays out central bank's instant payment framework"* (page 8)

5. *"Fed is expected to make a major commitment to ramping up inflation soon"* (page 10)

6. *"It is increasingly obvious to us that most economists are using the wrong lens to evaluate events"* (page 12)

7. China appears to be in the same fiscal predicament as the US (page 15)

8. Historically this has been a sign to buy gold and stocks, and sell USDs (page 16)

9. *"Now might be a good time to read up on the BIS's changes to gold's treatment as collateral..."* (page 18)

10. *"A demagogue, a product of one man's mental illness..." "No other president is going to do what I do"* (page 20)

Luke Gromen, CFA
FFTT, LLC
Info@FFTT-LLC.com
www.FFTT-LLC.com
Follow us on Twitter:
@LukeGromen

204

Made in the USA
Middletown, DE
24 August 2020